Richard Osman's HOUSE of GAMES

Richard Osman's HOUSE of GAMES

BBC BOOKS

1 3 5 7 9 10 8 6 4 2

BBC Books, an imprint of Ebury Publishing
20 Vauxhall Bridge Road,
London SW1V 2SA

BBC Books is part of the Penguin Random House group of companies
whose addresses can be found at global.penguinrandomhouse.com

Penguin
Random House
UK

First published by BBC Books in 2019
This edition published by BBC Books in 2019

www.penguin.co.uk

A CIP catalogue record for this book is available from the British Library

ISBN 9781785944628

Commissioning Editor: Yvonne Jacob
Editor: Charlotte Macdonald
Design: Clarkevanmeurs Ltd and E-type Design

Printed and bound in Great Britain by Clays Ltd, Elcograf S.p.A.

FSC www.fsc.org MIX Paper from responsible sources FSC® C018179

Penguin Random House is committed to a sustainable future for our business, our readers and our planet. This book is made from Forest Stewardship Council® certified paper.

CONTENTS

INTRODUCTION

RICHARD OSMAN: Hello there! You look great. Have you done something with your hair? Perhaps you've been working out? Either way, you're looking terrific.

Thank you so much for buying this book, even if it was heavily discounted. I promise you won't regret your decision. Although I should make it clear that this promise has no basis in financial or legal truth. Maybe you will regret it? I doubt it, but who knows? You're your own person, and how you react to this book is your own business. Please keep being you.

I think you probably *will* like this book though, and here's why.

Ahead of you are 101 different quizzes and games. Silly ones, funny ones, difficult ones, and frustratingly annoying ones which will re-open family rows that had lain dormant for years. It's all here!

I'm guessing you've watched *Richard Osman's House of Games* (or, as I call it, *My House of Games*) on TV? Otherwise why buy the book, right? So you know how it works. We invite four contestants to a little studio (hello Glasgow!), they play a whole series of different games, some games work really well, some games don't work at all, and then the middle-aged know-all in seat four wins.

It is a winning formula, and it has become so successful that they asked us to write a book, so that you could play *House of Games* at home. This is that book. You knew that, I know, I'm just covering all bases.

Now, *House of Games* has got the best question-writing team in the business. I spend a lot of time with them. There's the guy with the beard, there's Jane, or Joanne something, there's a woman who once drank a glass of milk in a meeting we had. (Who drinks milk in a meeting?) Also there are some other guys in lumberjack shirts and a woman with glasses. They are a great gang, and we get on tremendously well.

So this is what we decided to do. We're going to let you play some of our favourite *House of Games* games, with brand-new questions just for this book. For example, I have just finished writing a Christmas-themed Answer Smash for you. This is *exclusive content*, which is very important to the publishers.

We have also come up with lots of new rounds and lots of silly games for you to play. For each one we've tried to suggest the best ways to play them. Some work for teams, some for individuals, some need a quizmaster, and some are so hard they essentially need everyone to team up and get increasingly annoyed at each other.

Did I mention there are 101 of them? That is value for money right there. Depending on how much you paid, of course.

Now, you will notice that it is not only my name on the front cover. And that's because, as well as our wonderful question writers – Beardy, Milky and the rest of them – I have written this book with one of the great minds of his generation, Alan Connor, and, as I understand it, if he has his name on the cover, we don't have to pay him as much. It is great to have him on board.

Alan is, essentially, a genius. As well as writing questions for *House of Games* and being in charge of the questions on *Only Connect* for years, he has also written brilliant books about quizzing and about cryptic crosswords. I would mention the titles here, but they were probably for a different publisher. It's all politics.

Anyway, in a different generation Alan would be working at Bletchley Park, cracking the Enigma code. But, in the absence of Britain's involvement in a devastating global conflict, he works in light-entertainment television instead. Although, as I type, it strikes me that Alan could very well be a spy. He's the type, you know. I bet he is one, in fact. Either way, so long as it doesn't interfere with his work on this book, it is very much his business.

So, shall we press the buzzer and get on with the quizzes?

We love making *House of Games*, and I hope that comes across on screen. We have loved putting this book together too, and I hope that comes across on the page. Thank you so much for watching, and thank you so much for buying the book, and joining in the fun.

Enjoy the games, drink responsibly, and let us know how you get on.

Your pal,

Richard Osman, from *Richard Osman's House of Games*

ALAN CONNOR: Thank you, Richard. I am not a spy.* I have a few administrative notes, like the teacher at a nativity play who you ignore while they're pointing out the fire exits.

Just as evacuation routes are important, so is structure in quizzing. For each game, we've suggested the best number of players, whether someone should be appointed to read out the questions, and so on.

But it's your book now. Maybe you don't have the numbers suggested. Maybe you're reading this alone, in a spaceship. Feel free to ignore our suggestions and just see what works. Likewise, we suggest buzzers for some games. If you don't have buzzers, feel free to make your own with some electrical wire, a couple of 220-ohm resistors and a basic two-input OR gate. Or make animal noises.

If you want to keep score across all 101 games (that's over 1,000 questions at last count, almost all new to this book), we've provided a little scorecard at the end. Most importantly, some games will require you to use our patented (and perforated) House of Games Spoiler Blocker™ (also at the end), which you pull out and use to make sure no one jumps ahead, accidentally or otherwise.

Finally, you'll notice that some games, like Imaginary Charades and Three in Three, are ones where you could carry on playing, making up your own questions, after you've used our ones. In fact, we'd be delighted** if you did.

Your servant,

Alan Connor, also from *Richard Osman's House of Games*

---

* If you could see my face, you would know that I blurted that out in a startled way, not with the assured aplomb that a real spy would use to laugh off the charge. And that nervous response is actually *more* persuasive in telling you that I am not a spy. Or so they told me at MI6. When I was there researching a quiz.

** Legal department: please check how delighted.

GAMES

SET 1

... in which one of you might get impressively sweaty

GAME 1

THE FIRST-EVER ANSWER SMASH

You need: your House of Games Spoiler Blocker
Players: any number
Scoring: 2 points for every correct answer

AC: Now, this *is* an exciting start to a book. It's the questions from the first-ever time we played Answer Smash in the office. See how many you can get ...

RO: ... there's an 'and also' coming, I can feel it ...

AC: ... and also which of the Smashes we wouldn't allow nowadays on *House of Games*.

Below are some pictures of herbs and spices, each accompanied by a question. You have to give the answer which smashes both halves together.

1. Which Microsoft program was launched in 1995 and has a blue 'e' for its icon?

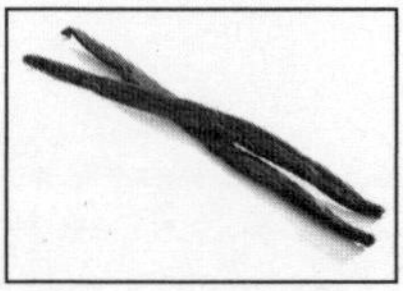

2. American state containing Chicago

3. Music-hall song adopted by West Ham fans

4. Its original title was 'The Landlord's Game'

5. Winners include Phil Tufnell and Carl 'Foggy' Fogarty

6. One-thousandth of a gigabyte

RO: Go on then, let's get this over with. Which would we not be 'allowed' to use on the show?

AC: Vanillinois, Star Anise Up *and* Thyme a Celebrity. This was from the wild, chaotic days before we established the rule that the overlapping parts have to be spelled the same.

RO: I hadn't noticed. And when I do Answer Smashes for events, like the World Snooker backstage party, I don't follow that rule. In fact, I'm not sure I've even followed it in this book.

AC: I had noticed.

Answers: 1 Minternet Explorer 2 Vanillinois 3 Star Anise Up Mother Brown 4 Cinnamonopoly 5 Thyme a Celebrity ... Get Me Out of Here! 6 Nutmegabyte

GAME 2

A DISTINCTLY AVERAGE CHRISTMAS

You need: pencil and paper; a phone, or someone who's good with numbers
Players: 4, 6, 8, 10 ... basically, an even number that's 4 or more
Scoring: 2 points for every win

RO: You know how Distinctly Average works. You team up with a partner. We ask a question that you couldn't possibly know the actual answer to, but to which you might be able to make an educated guess. You write down your answer, which you are fairly confident about.

Your partner also writes down their answer, which is usually terrible. You then take the average score as your team's answer.* It's really, really, really, really, really, really important to pick a good partner in this round. Your mum's friend from work who popped over for drinks, and now won't leave, is just not going to cut it. Try Auntie Julia, she's clever.

AC: This is something that Clara Amfo learned when Nish Kumar overestimated the average cost of Christmas for a household (the answer is £809.97; Nish went for £10,000, later remarking that 'Hindu Christmases are really extravagant').

RO: Anyway, I've come up with ten Christmassy questions. Take your time, really think things through, and then panic and write down something plainly ridiculous.

---

* Add them together and halve the result, but you knew that.

1. According to US scientists, how many miles per hour does Santa have to travel, if he is to deliver to all the relevant homes in the world in one day?

2. A New York family holds the world record for the most ever Christmas lights on a residential property. How many lights did they have?

3. The first ever commercially sold Christmas cards appeared in 1843. One sold at auction in 2014. For how much?

4. How many rolls of Sellotape were sold in the UK in December 2018?

5. If you add up all of the presents my true love sent to me in the song 'The Twelve Days of Christmas', how many presents would you have in total?

6. Christmas is all about Jesus or Santa, depending on your preference. What is the distance in miles from the North Pole to Bethlehem?

7. As recorded on the BBC News site in 2018, what is the population of Turkey?

8. And what's the population of Brussels?

9. How many Christmas trees did Brits buy in 2018?

10. According to the Met Office, how many times has a snowflake fallen somewhere in the UK on Christmas Day in the last 54 years?

Answers: 1. 2,340,000mph 2. 601,736 lights 3. £8,469 (excluding postage) 4. 6 million rolls 5. 364 gifts (it's the 12th triangular number!) 6. 4,034 miles 7. 79.5 million Turks 8. 1.2 million Bruxellois 9. 8 million trees 10. 38

GAME 3
IMAGINARY CHARADES #1

You need: your House of Games Spoiler Blocker
Players: any number; make 2 teams or just take it in turns to act out the titles
Scoring: 20 points for whoever has made the bravest choices and moves

Charades is a pleasant enough way of whiling away some time. But as anyone who has played it can tell you, there's one big problem. The books and songs that you're trying to mime to everyone else: well, they're all real.

For one thing, this is boring. For another, all a player has to convey is 'film, four words, third word eyes' and it's obviously *For Your Eyes Only*. Way too easy, right?

This time, you'll be playing charades the *House of Games* way. Block off the titles below. The first player will move the House of Games Spoiler Blocker to reveal the first title; the next player is either someone from the other team (if you're doing teams) or whoever got the answer first.

TITLES

(younger players: if you don't know some of the names and words, just make up your own title instead)

1. Salad Wars (film)
2. The Forgetful Stegosaurus (book)
3. Ninety-Nine Press-Ups (song)
4. The Repugnant Australians (play)
5. Salad Wars II: The Caper Caper (film)
6. I'm in the Red, So I'm Singin' the Blues (song)
7. Britain's Wettest Pets (TV show)
8. Tulips from my Aunt (book)
9. Fifty-five Miles from Durham (song)
10. Salad Wars III: Lettuce Get Ready to Rumble (film)

GAME 4

SEE MY GUESTS #1&2

You need: your House of Games Spoiler Blocker
Players: any number (and someone to check your guesses)
Scoring: see below

RO: One thing that *House of Games* guests especially enjoy is the avatar we make of their face for our game board.

AC: Yes! And it struck me that we could turn them into quiz.

RO: A lot of things strike you as having quiz potential, Alan. Remember that time an amp crushed the sound guy's foot and you went to the Glasgow Royal Infirmary to 'cheer him up' with an Answer Smash about the bones he'd broken?

AC: Metatarsalisbury Cathedral, classic.* But if we're going to ask the readers to identify the avatars, I've realised there's some we can't use.

RO: Because they're based on hairdo, eyewear and facial hair, you mean, and some contestants, very stylishly, don't have any of those?

AC: Tom Allen. Just a pair of sassy eyebrows.

In this game, you work together.

---

* Looking back, this was actually really inappropriate. The 'sal' in 'metatarsal' and 'Salisbury' are pronounced completely differently.

You'll see two images of guests from the TV version of *House of Games*. If you can tell who they are straightaway, that's *10 points each*. (Get someone else to check, in case you're wrong.)

If you can't, then there are some nice straightforward questions underneath, of the kind we use in our round It's All In The Name. As that name suggests, this will give you some of the letters of the guest's name. But each time you use one of these questions, *the points available go down by 2*.

Cooperation and inspiration: and you'll all boost your scores.

Exciting note: for some guests, we create multiple avatars. Here we reserve the right to use our 'out-take avatars', partly to keep you on your toes and partly to give you another thrilling peek behind *House of Games*'s velvet ropes.

GUEST ONE

For 10 points:

Can you name her?

Answer these questions to get some of the letters in her name.

For 8 points:

First name of the actor who has played roles with first names including Lenny, Carl, Mumbles, Benjamin … and Dorothy

Answer: Dustin

For 6 points:

Day falling roughly in the middle of the month in the Roman calendar

Answer: Ides

For 4 points:

Type of beach opened in Brighton in 1980

Answer: Nudist

For 2 points:

First name of Los Angeles road that stretches from Figueroa to the Pacific Coast Highway

Answer: Sunset

Answer: Susie Dent

GUEST TWO

For 10 points:

Can you name him?

Answer these questions to get some of the letters in his name.

For 8 points:

French word which describes a combination of tiredness, sadness and boredom

Answer: Ennui

For 6 points:

2016 television drama starring Geoffrey Rush as Albert Einstein

Answer: Genius

For 4 points:

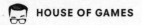

1996 film starring Geoffrey Rush as David Helfgott

Answer: Shine

For 2 points:

Classic Frank Herbert sci-fi novel adapted for film by David Lynch in 1984

Answer: Dune

Answer: Hugh Dennis

SET 1 SCORECARD				
	Player 1	Player 2	Player 3	Player 4
Game 1				
Game 2				
Game 3				
Game 4				
Totals				

WINNER! ______________________________

SET 2

... for which you may choose to change out of your favourite jumper

GAME 1

THE TENSE WATER-PISTOL GAME

You need: a water pistol, pencil, paper (If you don't approve of replica firearms, squirty toys are available in the shape of seahorses, dragons and so on ... or you could use a washing-up bottle, though you really should probably rinse out the detergent first)

Players: 3 or more

Scoring: 10 points for whoever is driest at the end, to be agreed by popular vote or argument

When it's your turn to hold the water pistol, take a look at the list of categories below. Choose one and read it out, then secretly write down something that fits that category.

Now, go round the other players in turn. Aim the water pistol at their face and ask them to name something in that category. If it's not what you wrote down, they're safe (for now) and you move on to the next player.

But: don't move on too quickly. They might blurt out an answer quickly, but you can take your time. Make them wait. Fix their gaze. Make them sweat. Enjoy yourself.

And, of course, when someone *does* say what you wrote down, let them have it. Both barrels. Don't hold back. Because they won't when it's their turn - which is now.

CATEGORIES

Countries beginning with 'I'

Fruit

James Bond films

Colours

Colours of the rainbow

People who have played the Doctor in *Doctor Who*

Shops on your nearest high street

Channels available on your TV

Nursery rhymes

Or add your own

For extra tension, play the same category repeatedly as a test of memory and nerve.

GAME 2

RHYME TIME

You need: your House of Games Spoiler Blocker
Players: someone to read, and 2 or more players
Scoring: see below

You know Rhyme Time. You get a pair of clues. There's a pair of answers. And the answers rhyme. Douglas Hurd; lemon curd. Gordon Brown; *Watership Down*. And some that don't involve political figures of yesteryear.

If you're reading, choose someone to get the first pair of clues. Two points if they get both right; if not, pass it to the right for 1 point until someone does.

Then play passes to the right.

1. **Game Boris Johnson claimed was 'invented on the dining tables of England'**

   Answer: Ping-pong

   Words preceding 'The Witch is Dead' and 'Merrily on High' in song titles

   Answer: Ding Dong

2. **Striker with record for the most headed goals in the Premier League**

   Answer: Peter Crouch

   Nose-less, misanthropic, bin-dwelling citizen of *Sesame Street*

   Answer: Oscar the Grouch

3. **Song performed with two drummers at Live Aid**

   Answer: 'Stairway to Heaven'

   Three to the power three

   Answer: Twenty-seven

4. **Section of the A4 that's home to the Royal Academy and Fortnum & Mason**

   Answer: Piccadilly

   Act whose 1990 Grammy for Best New Artist was nullified

   Answer: Milli Vanilli

5. **Common name for the medical condition *varicella***

   Answer: Chickenpox

   Star of both *Scream* and *Friends*

   Answer: Courtenay Cox

6. **Baked good named after the shape of the moon**

   Answer: Croissant

   Smiths song covered by Slow Moving Millie for a John Lewis ad

   Answer: 'Please, Please, Please, Let Me Get What I Want'

7. **Mythical creature often depicted as a shoemaker**

   Answer: Leprechaun

   Forgetful spy played by Matt Damon

   Answer: Jason Bourne

8. **Theatre featured in Hitchcock's *The 39 Steps***

   Answer: London Palladium

   London's Live Aid Venue

   Answer: Wembley Stadium

9. **What potassium bitartrate is called by bakers**

   Answer: Cream of tartar

   Document of political and personal liberty signed by King John in 1215

   Answer: Magna Carta

10. **Comics character who first appeared in 1951**

    Answer: Dennis the Menace

    Sport referred to in the first question

    Answer: Table tennis

GAME 3
THREE IN THREE

You need: a phone with a stopwatch
Players: any number
Scoring: 1 point for every successful triplet of answers

The rules are simple. Take it in turns to answer.

When it's your turn, another player reads out a category from the lists below and immediately presses START on a stopwatch.

If you say three things in that category in three seconds, you get a point. Then it's someone else's turn.

We're suggesting some categories for the grown-ups and others for the youngsters, but you can ignore that if you like, especially if the grown-ups aren't as smart as the youngsters. Or you can ignore all of them and make up your own categories.

Settle any challenges using Wikipedia. We'd give the answers here, but there are thousands of them; also, the way the world is today, there may be different countries by the time we go to press. If they can strip the luckless Pluto of its planet status, who knows what can happen?

YOUNGSTERS	GROWN-UPS
South American countries	South American capital cities
Planets in our solar system	The three furthest planets in our solar system
Metals in the periodic table	Elements which are gases at room temperature
TV nature shows	Sitcoms which aired in the 1970s
Kings who have ruled England	Queens who have ruled England (not including Elizabeths)
Parts of the intestinal system	Parts of the eye
Rodents	Marsupials
Beatles songs	Solo Beatles songs
Actors who've played the Doctor in *Doctor Who*	Actors who've played assistants in *Doctor Who*
Wives of Henry VIII	Kings before William the Conqueror
UK newspapers	Foreign newspapers
Square numbers	Prime numbers
British rivers	American rivers
National flags featuring the colour blue	National flags featuring the colour green
Members of the current England men's football squad	Members of the current French men's football squad
Tom Cruise movies	Tom Hardy movies
Four-sided shapes	Types of triangle
Shakespeare plays	Oscar Wilde plays
Cluedo suspects	Items to remove in *Operation*
Categories already played	Answers an opponent has given

GAME 4
CHRISTMAS SMASH

You need: nothing
Players: 2 or more, plus someone to read aloud the Smashes
Scoring: 1 for each correct smash

RO: Many people holding this book will have given or received it as a Christmas present, in a desperate attempt to stop their entire family simply drinking and scrolling through their phones throughout the festive period. To celebrate that attempt, doomed though it is, here is a selection of specially themed Christmas Answer Smashes. As Alan has no doubt explained elsewhere ...

AC: ... to be precise, in Game #1, when we shared the very first Answer Smash ...

RO: ... there are very strict rules as to what can and can't be an Answer Smash question. Fortunately, I am too old for rules now.

AC: Wait, what?

RO: That's right. Let's forget the rules. As my Christmas present.

AC: We could *temporarily* waive the minimum two-letter overlap, I suppose, but ...

RO: Listen, Alan: I've written a set, and some of them don't even have the same letters in the Smash bit. They just sound good.

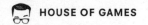

AC: I … see. Can we do another set later? One that does follow all the rules?

RO: OK, we'll slavishly follow the 'rules' next time. As your Christmas present.

The questions come in pairs. You give both parts, smashed together. So if the clues were 'Cylindrical Christmas treat' and 'Rugby union terrace chant', you would smash YULE LOG into OGGY OGGY OGGY OI OI OI and give the answer: YULE LOGGY OGGY OGGY OI OI OI.

1	Type of song traditionally sung at Christmas	Rachel Riley's predecessor on *Countdown*
2	President of Russia	Something you use to decorate the Christmas tree
3	What pigs love to eat	The star of the greatest ever Christmas film, *Elf*
4	Australian soap which began in 1988	The Christmas song with a line 'The cattle are lowing …'
5	Where Jesus was born	A sport, also known as ping-pong
6	A disgusting Christmas dinner vegetable	Where we had to go to the loo before indoor plumbing

7	How Santa laughs	1984 Christmas film starring Macaulay Culkin
8	Incredibly annoying song about a sea creature	Christmas song which includes the line 'Glory to the new-born King'
9	A mixture of eggs, flour and water, served at any self-respecting Christmas dinner	Where the Great Fire of London began
10	Prince single, released in 1984	The creatures used to pull Santa's sleigh
11	Gifts given by the Three Wise Men	Agatha Christie mystery, set on a train
12	Small orange sometimes found in Christmas stockings	Star of *Pulp Fiction* and *Kill Bill*
13	King who looked out on the Feast of Stephen	US city, the name of which translates as 'The Meadows'
14	Novelty hit single with a prominent pineapple	A Christmas number 1, three times, for Band Aid
15	TV show where people get paid for sitting around, watching telly	The day when you eat turkey sandwiches and wish your relatives would leave

16	Christmas song about two types of plant	A group of American universities, including Harvard and Yale
17	What you end up with bags full of on Christmas Day	Teenage job killed off by the internet
18	A type of butter you might have with Christmas pudding	British Wimbledon champion
19	Britain's busiest airport	A Christmas chocolate assortment
20	The Christmas plant known in Latin as Viscum album	The US band who had a hit with one of the greatest songs of all time, 'Africa'

Answers: 1. (Christmas) Carol Vorderman 2. Vladimir Putinsel 3. Swill Ferrell 4. Home and Away in a Manger 5. Stable Tennis 6. Brussel(s) sprouthouse/sproutside loo, etc. 7. Ho Ho Home Alone 8. Baby Shark the Herald Angels Sing* 9. Yorkshire Pudding Lane 10. Purple Raindeer 11. Gold, Frankincense and Myrrhder on the Orient Express 12. Satsuma Thurman 13. Wenceslas Vegas 14. Agadoo They Know It's Christmas? 15. Goggleboxing Day 16. The Holly and the Ivy League 17. Wrapping Paper Round 18. Brandy Murray 19. Heathrowses 20. Mistletoeto**

* 'Baby Shark' went big in 2017, but its origin is a campfire song of the 1970s inspired by *Jaws*.

** 'Africa' by Mistletoeto is so good, in fact, it even gives good quiz: see Game Game 2, Page 87: Win When They're Singing

SET 2 SCORECARD				
	Player 1	Player 2	Player 3	Player 4
Game 1				
Game 2				
Game 3				
Game 4				
Totals				

WINNER!

SET 3

... in which you may wish you hadn't been the first to answer

GAME 1

FINGERS OFF BUZZERS #1

You need: a buzzer or other piece of noise-making equipment each
Players: any number, plus someone to read things out
Scoring: see below

The rules here are simple: every time you're the first to buzz with a correct answer, you get a point, *but* if the correct answer begins with the Letter of Doom, you lose all your points so far. (That's 'so far' as in during a session of Fingers Off Buzzers, not 'so far' as in 'during your lifetime'. We're not monsters.) That applies even if you don't give an answer; you only have to buzz to get the penalty.

Person reading out: we've put an asterisk next to the Letter of Doom answers, and given you a Richard Osman-style friendly introduction so that no one can complain that they don't understand what they've been asked to do. *Keep up the pace* to trick them into blurting out an answer.

'I'll read out a historic county, you buzz in and tell me its county town. The Letter of Doom is ... S.'

Berkshire (Reading)

Avon (Bristol)

County Fermanagh (Enniskillen)

Cheshire (Chester)

Herefordshire (Hereford)

Hertfordshire (Hertford)

Staffordshire (Stafford)*

Kent (Maidstone)

Shetland (Lerwick)

Cornwall (Truro)

Shropshire (Shrewsbury)*

Buckinghamshire (Aylesbury)

Bedfordshire (Bedford)

Kirkcudbrightshire (Kirkcudbright)

Selkirkshire (Selkirk)*

Glamorgan (Cardiff)

Stirlingshire (Stirling)*

Essex (Chelmsford)

County Tyrone (Omagh)

Cumberland (Carlisle)

Norfolk (Norwich)

Devon (Exeter)

GAME 2
AND THE ANSWER ISN'T #1

You need: a smartphone or tablet; your House of Games Spoiler Blocker

Players: ideally 4; you could make it work with 2 but it's probably not worth it

Scoring: see below

These four questions are multiple-choice, but we haven't bothered to come up with the wrong ones. That's your job.

When it's your turn, everyone else looks at the question and its answer. Then (so that handwriting is no clue), someone takes the phone and types in (in random order) the right answer and a multi-choice option from each of the other players. (You shouldn't also type in any of the fun facts we offer as explanation.)

Then you get the phone, someone reads you the question, and you consider the options.

If you're right, you get a point. Obviously. But if you're wrong, the point goes to whoever invented the option you chose. Take your time ...

1. **How many countries are in the G20?**

   Answer: 19 (the '20th' is the EU)

2. **Why is a converted aircraft hangar in the remote Canadian town Churchill, Manitoba, a dangerous place to work?**

   Answer: It is a prison for polar bears (the bears' migration route mean that after months of eating berries and seaweed, they pass through Churchill when they are their hungriest)

3. **What was the original name of the band Coldplay?**

   Answer: Starfish

4. **What enviable property is possessed by the small translucent jellyfish known to science as *Turritopsis dohrnii*?**

   Answer: Immortality (it is the 'Immortal Jellyfish', which can revert to a sexually immature stage of life, and grow up again; the fact that it can keep doing so indefinitely makes it 'biologically immortal')

GAME 3

PROJECTED IMAGE NOMENCLATURE CHALLENGE

You need: nothing
Players: 2 or more (plus 1 to read out the questions)
Scoring: 2 points for every correct answer

RO: Sometimes, when films are released in other countries, their titles are changed. This famously happened when *The Madness of George III* was released in America as *The Madness of King George* because US film bosses were concerned that audiences might think they'd missed the first two films in the series.

Other times, the titles are translated into the local language. I'm giving you some of my favourite examples and we want the original titles. They're all famous films.

Some are quite clever, some are very bad literal translations, some contain some fairly major spoilers, and a couple are, frankly, incomprehensible. If any of you get no. 10 or no. 12, then I take my hat off to you.

1. *The Teeth from the Sea* - France
2. *Imaginary Dead Baseball Players Live in My Cornfield* - Hong Kong
3. *We Are Newscasters* - Japan
4. *Knight of the Night* - Spain
5. *The Happy Dumpling to Be, Who Talks, and Solves Agricultural Problems* - Hong Kong
6. *Vaseline* - Argentina
7. *Mom, I Missed the Plane!* - France
8. *Austin Powers, The Spy Who Behaved Very Nicely Around Me* - Malaysia
9. *Santa Is a Pervert* - Czech Republic
10. *Super Power Dare Die Team* - China
11. *Wild Speed* - Japan
12. *The Young People Who Traverse Dimensions While Wearing Sunglasses* - France
13. *Rita Hayworth, Key to Escape* - Finland
14. *He's a Ghost* - China
15. *It's Raining Falafel* - Israel
16. *American Virgin Man* - China

17. *Go, with Bath!* - China

18. *The Rebel Novice Nun* - Mexico

19. *Bloody Oil* - Italy

20. *I Will Marry a Prostitute to Save Money* - China

Answers: 1. *Jaws* 2. *Field of Dreams* 3. *Anchorman 2: The Legend Continues* 4. *The Dark Knight* 5. *Babe* 6 *Grease* 7. *Home Alone* 8. *Austin Powers: The Spy Who Shagged Me* 9. *Bad Santa* 10. *Ghostbusters* 11. *The Fast and the Furious* 12. *The Matrix* 13. *The Shawshank Redemption* 14. *The Sixth Sense* 15. *Cloudy with a Chance of Meatballs* 16. *American Pie* 17. *Hot Tub Time Machine* 18. *The Sound of Music* 19. *There Will Be Blood* 20. *Pretty Woman*

GAME 4

NO-WORDS GEOGRAPHY

You need: a pencil
Players: any number
Scoring: none, this is a fun interlude (or give 5 points to whoever first gets no. 3 if you're irredeemably competitive)

Take your time with this one, and think laterally.

Work in a team to match the pictures to the place names on the map.

For example, if there were a picture of a hip-hop posse, and a number positioned in east Cheshire on the map, you would match CREW and CREWE (giving both answers). The actual questions are more ... playful.

Feel free to write on the map, or you can use a separate sheet of paper if you prefer.*

* If you're trying to keep the book pristine thinking that it might one day become valuable, it won't - unless it's signed, and by signed we mean by all four Beatles.

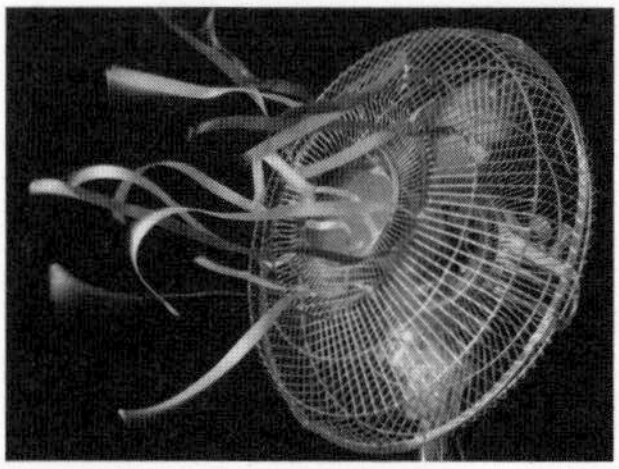

W.C.

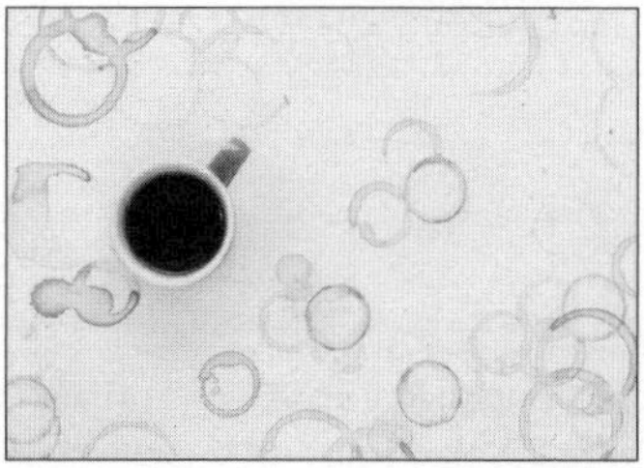

Answers: 1. Skye / Sky 2. Ayr / Air 3. Durham / Durum 4. Leeds / Leads 5. Bury / Berry 6. Keele / Keel 7. Towcester / Toaster 8. Staines / Stains 9. Cowes / Cows 10. Looe / Loo

SET 3 SCORECARD				
	Player 1	Player 2	Player 3	Player 4
Game 1				
Game 2				
Game 3				
Game 4				
Totals				

WINNER!

SET 4

... in which you must try your hardest NOT to sing

GAME 1

FINGERS OFF BUZZERS #2

You need: a buzzer or other piece of noise-making equipment each
Players: any number, plus someone to read things out
Scoring: see below

The rules here are simple: every time you're the first to buzz with a correct answer, you get a point, *but* if the correct answer begins with the Letter of Doom, you lose all your points so far. That applies even if you don't give an answer; you only have to buzz to get the penalty.

Person reading out: we've put an asterisk next to the Letter of Doom answers, and given you a Richard Osman-style friendly introduction so that no one can complain that they don't understand what they've been asked to do. Keep up the pace to trick them into blurting out an answer.

'Complete the following sums. The Letter of Doom is ... F.'

8 × 11 (88)

14 ÷ 2 (7)

14 ÷ 7 (2)

7 × 2 (14)*

110 ÷ 2 (55)*

44 × 0 (0)

84 ÷ 7 (12)

96 ÷ 12 (8)

7 × 8 (56)*

11 × 11 (121)

223 × 2 (446)*

99 × 3 (297)

454 ÷ 2 (227)

17 × 3 (51)*

55 × 3 (165)

6 × 8 (48)*

11 × 12 (132)

GAME 2
BROKEN KARAOKE #1

You need: nothing
Players: 2 or more (plus one to read out the questions)
Scoring: 2 points for every correct answer

AC: What's the best match we've had of game to contestant?

RO: I'd have to go back the first episode we broadcast. Clara Amfo and Broken Karaoke. She nailed it, then we played it again at the end of the week and she was again an absolute monster. Any genre, any period of pop music. It was wonderful to watch.

AC: Not for Al Murray, Nish Kumar and Anneka Rice, it wasn't.

RO: Yes, but you know what? I think it was good for Al's soul.

If you're reading the questions, first give the year. Then read out the initials to the lyrics from a well-known passage in a well-known pop song. Try to match them how the song sounds (e.g. if the song contains a very long 'yeeeeeeeeaaaaaaaaaaaaah', say a simple 'Y', then wait until giving the next letter).

TRY TO STAY ON ONE NOTE. This is not a game about melody. It's pure words, all the way.

If you don't know a song, skip it (or give it your best shot).

And if they don't get it the first time, just read it again ...

1 Year: 1984

ITSS
IYN
WYGC
G
ITSW
AIDLG
WYGC
G

2 Year: 1978

BGITR
TLLLL
TABGITR
TLLLLL
BGITR
TLLLL
SLLASIAP
PP

3 Year: 2014

CUFGGITY
CUFGGITY
CUFGGITY
SNAWITS
DBMJW(CO)
DBMJW
DBMJW
DBMJW
DBMJW
DBMJW
HHHO

4 Year: 1985

IWOS
(W)
IWOS
(W)
IWOS
(W)
ADIFG

5 Year: 2000

WLTDO
(WWWWW)
WLTDO
(WWWWW)
WLTDO
(WWWWW)
WLTDO

Answers: 1. 'Ghostbusters' 2. 'Brown Girl in the Ring' 3. 'Uptown Funk' 4. 'Walking on Sunshine' 5. 'Who Let the Dogs Out?'

GAME 3

YOU'VE GOT TO HAVE A CATCHPHRASE

You need: nothing
Players: any number
Scoring: none; work together until you've got them all (all right, if you're feeling really competitive, 1 point each)

RO: Here are the initials of some well loved British comedy catchphrases with the characters who say them and the year each was first broadcast. (How much more information do you need? I can't do the whole thing for you.) I want you to give *the initials of the names of the shows.*

I, of course, have one of the catchiest catchphrases on British television. 'And by "country", I mean a sovereign state that is recognised by the United Nations in its own right.' You hear this a lot in school playgrounds up and down the country.

I would play this as a team round if I were you, as they take a while to work out. I can pretty much guarantee that no one will get all 20. I can also guarantee that if someone *does* get all 20, then they'll let me know on Twitter.

1. **YSB - Capt. M (1968)**

2. **YBNBYBNB - VP (2003)**

3. **DMTW - BF (1975)**

4. **GB? - BP (2001)**

5. H-D-HC! - GP (1980)

6. KMKYA-H - AP (1992)

7. IF - Mr. H (1972)

8. NNNNNNY - JT (1994)

9. TTNYWBM - DT (1981)

10. AIB? - L (2004)

11. LVCISSTOO (or, indeed, LVCISSZOO) - MD (1982)

12. IDBI - VM (1990)

13. YDOM! - HS (1962)

14. TIALSFLP - E and T (1999)

15. IHACP - B (1983)

16. MA - JR (1998)

17. OB - FS (1973)

18. OYAABILY - M (1963)

19. IGFM ... AIGFH - RB and RC (1971)

20. WO? - NJ (2007)

Answers: 1. DA (*Dad's Army*) 2. LB (*Little Britain*) 3. FT (*Fawlty Towers*) 4. PN (*Phoenix Nights*) 5. H-D-H (*Hi-de-Hi!*) 6. KMKYWAP (*Knowing Me, Knowing You with Alan Partridge*) 7. AYBS? (*Are You Being Served?*) 8. TVOD (*The Vicar of Dibley*) 9. OFAH (*Only Fools and Horses*) 10. TCTS (*The Catherine Tate Show*) 11. A!A! (*'Allo! 'Allo!*) 12. OFITG (*One Foot in the Grave*) 13. SAS (*Steptoe and Son*) 14. TLOG (*The League of Gentlemen*) 15. B (*Blackadder*) 16. TRF (*The Royle Family*) 17. SMDAE (*Some Mothers Do 'Ave 'Em*) 18. TDES (*The Dick Emery Show*) 19. TTR (*The Two Ronnies*) 20. G&S (*Gavin & Stacey*)

GAME 4
YOU COMPLETE ME

You need: buzzers or some kind of noise-makers
Players: 4 (plus someone to read things out)
Scoring: 2 points for every correct answer

AC: This game is perfect for people who know how to finish each other's ...

AC: ... don't leave me hanging ...

AC: ... Richard?

Get into pairs. No, you can't all go with Clever Cousin Connie, who's been predicted all A-stars.

All set?

If you're the one reading out the questions, rest assured it's because of your compelling and sonorous tones. They were talking about someone else when they used the words 'points desert'.

And since you are the one reading them out, here's how it goes. All the answers have two words. Whoever buzzes first can only give the first word – and their partner earns each of them 2 points *only* if they can successfully give the *second* word.

(If they don't you can pass it over, and don't let on if the first word was wrong: keep things exciting even if there are no points at stake.)

1. **Which monarch does Olivia Colman play in *The Favourite*?**

   Answer: Queen Anne

2. **What is the capital of El Salvador?**

   Answer: San Salvador

3. **Who is the patron saint of travellers?**

   Answer: Saint Christopher

4. **What is the name of the orphan protagonist in the Charles Dickens's novel *Great Expectations*?**

   Answer: Pip (or Philip) Pirrip

5. **Which 2005 film was the first to star Christian Bale as Bruce Wayne?**

   Answer: *Batman Begins*

6. **Who is the Toytown police officer in Enid Blyton's Noddy stories?**

   Answer: Mr Plod

7. **What is the first name and surname of Declan Donnelly's usual presenting partner?**

   Answer: Anthony McPartlin

8. **What was the title of the first book to be written by children's author Roger Hargreaves?**

   Answer: *Mr Tickle*

9. **In which Shakespeare play is England referred to as a sceptred isle?**

   Answer: *Richard II*

10. Which soft, chewy sweet was introduced to the market by Rowntree's in 1965?

Answer: Jelly Tots (Jelly Babies were probably invented in 1864, and originally sold as 'Unclaimed Babies'; jelly beans were also invented around the end of the nineteenth century)

SET 4 SCORECARD				
	Player 1	Player 2	Player 3	Player 4
Game 1				
Game 2				
Game 3				
Game 4				
Totals				

WINNER!

SET 5

... in which it may help to have an age in single digits

GAME 1

IT'S ALL IN RICHARD'S NAME

You need: something to buzz in with
Players: any number, plus someone to read them out
Scoring: 1 point for every correct answer

RO: Our guests are always tickled to find what words we can make from the letters of their names.

AC: It makes me think of when Louis XIII appointed an *Anagrammatiste Royale* to discover people's characters by jumbling their names.

RO: And sometimes we get an answer that sounds a bit rude.

AC: Richard, I've always thought it's a pity we haven't done *your* name. It's unusually fecund. There are even some full anagrams! Try this clue: 'Poldark, say, or Doc Martin'.

RO: Hang on ... Got it. CORNISH DRAMA.

AC: Yep. 'Set for a low-budget theatre production'.

RO: One moment, please ... RANDOM CHAIRS.

AC: And, 'Question you'd consider before boxing with President Emmanuel'.

RO: ... which also sounds a bit rude. I'll leave the readers to puzzle it out.

NB: these ones are not full anagrams, but they can all be made from RICHARD OSMAN.

1. **Pasta mentioned in 'Yankee Doodle Dandy'**

2. **The first lucky lady to be serenaded by Lou Bega in the chorus of his 'Mambo No 5'**

3. **Musical instruments with twenty reeds**

4. **Musical instruments that are even more child-friendly than the previous ones**

5. **American president referred to in title of the drama *Mad Men***

6. **European country with more or less the same population as Chester**

7. **A creature that drinks your dog's blood, a black widow, and the animal in David Dimbleby's tattoo are all examples**

8. **Bitter liqueur whose non-alcoholic imitation is part of the mocktail Shirley Temple**

9. **State capital of Virginia, named after a town in south-west London, named after a castle in Yorkshire, named after a town in Normandy whose name means 'splendid hill'**

10. **Friend to Stevie, daughter to Penny, frenemy to Tilly**

Answers: 1. Macaroni (in those days, macaroni were dumplings; the word was also used to mean 'posh') 2. Monica 3. Harmonicas (indeed, some strange harmonicas may have more or fewer than 10) 4. Ocarinas 5. Madison ('Mad Men' are the advertising execs of Madison Avenue) 6. Andorra ('same population' as in size, not the people themselves) 7. Arachnids (accept arachnoids; Dimbleby's scorpion has six legs, but he decided to leave it be, remarking 'I'm no David Attenborough') 8. Maraschino (in the cherry; NB: Italians say maraSKino, not maraSHino) 9. Richmond 10. Miranda

GAME 2

5, 6, 7, 8

You need: a phone each (pencil and paper for anyone that's on less than 20 per cent battery); Steps' breakthrough single '5, 6, 7, 8' to play in the background (optional)

Players: any number

Scoring: 20 points for whoever wins most often

The rules of this game are very few.

But that does not make it a simple game. The potential for tactical play is immense. So is the potential for manipulating the minds of your fellow players. So is the potential for recriminations. Enjoy!

Each player takes out his or her phone (a calculator app is handy for this, with its nice big display) and taps one of the numbers 5, 6, 7 or 8.

Once everyone has done that, the player with the lowest number *that no one else has tapped in* is the winner.

If there is no winner, play again. If there is a winner, play again.

And again. And again.

GAME 3

ANSWER SMASH – FAMOUS MOUSTACHES

You need: your House of Games Spoiler Blocker
Players: any number
Scoring: 2 points for every correct answer

Remember, no points unless you smash the answers together ...

Block off the questions, gather round and yell when you've got the answer.

The title of which Mozart composition is often translated, with questionable accuracy, as 'A Little Night Music'?

Answer: Albert Einsteine Kleine Nachtmusik

Who played the title character in the 1966 film *Georgy Girl?*

Answer: Errol Flynn Redgrave

Which country legend performed with Alison Krauss and Gillian Welch on the soundtrack to *O Brother, Where Art Thou?*

Answer: Lemmylou Harris

Which former member of Oasis released 'Wall of Glass' and 'Paper Crown' as a solo artist?

Answer: Salvador Daliam Gallagher

Hindus regard which river as holy?

Answer: Hulk Hoganges

What baffling film of 2010 starred Leonardo DiCaprio and Marion Cotillard?

Answer: Prinception

Diamondback and sidewinder are both species of what?

Answer: Borattlesnake

What film stars Bruce Willis as a police officer protecting a young boy who has cracked an 'unbreakable' code?

Answer: Freddie Mercury Rising

The dissolution of the monasteries was the idea of which monarch?

Answer: Ben E. King Henry VIII

What range separates the Eastern Seaboard from the interior of North America?

Answer: Frank Zappalachian Mountains

GAME 4

GENERATION VS GENERATION

You need: clear voices
Players: any number, plus 2 people to read out the clues
Scoring: 1 point for every correct answer

RO: We weren't allowed to give it a name based on *The Generation Game*, then?

AC: Nope. And they've said we can't do the game where we give the answers and they have to come up with questions about big cats.

RO: Shame. I've just written a fantastic new question set for *Leopardy*.

This is a game for two generations, so split into groups (either or both can be a group of one).

Get the 2 clue-readers gathered together holding this book. Now whichever of you is taller, read out this explanation:

'We're going to read two questions at the same time, one for the younger players and one for the older. The answers are the same. Shout out as many guesses as you can think of. I will be deciding quickly who gave the right answer first, so make sure you are as [shout this bit] LOUD AS POSSIBLE.'

THE OCTONAUTS

The answers are all characters from *The Octonauts*, but the questions for older players are not about Octonauts.

YOUNGER: Which Octonaut likes xylophones, works as a medic, and is a penguin who shouts 'flappity flippers'?

OLDER: From a word meaning 'weight' in Spanish, what is the currency of Chile, Colombia and Cuba?

Answer: Peso

YOUNGER: Which character founded the Octonauts and is an octopus and professor who likes to say 'fascinating'?

OLDER: J.R.R. Tolkien and C.S. Lewis were part of a book group named after what word, meaning a vague idea?

Answer: Inkling

YOUNGER: Which brave Octonaut works as the captain, does the driving and is a polar bear who shouts 'to the launch bay!'?

OLDER: Cirripedology is the study of what kind of marine arthropod?

Answer: Barnacles

MR MEN

The answers are all surnames of Mr Men, but the questions for older players are not about Mr Men.

YOUNGER: Which of the Mr Men is pink and scribbly and is taught by a kindly tramp to count to ten when he feels scared?

OLDER: Since the eighteenth century, a calf's foot has been combined with hot water to make which ingredient of trifle?

Answer: Jelly

YOUNGER: Which of the yellow Mr Men has a big red nose and a green hat and sleeps in a rowing boat?

OLDER: What sort of verse, popular in the nineteenth century, is associated with Lewis Carroll and Edward Lear?

Answer: Nonsense

YOUNGER: Which of the Mr Men is red and square, puts out a fire in a cornfield, and is rewarded with eggs?

OLDER: Which 1999 Robbie Williams single was his attempt to persuade fans that he sometimes needed some privacy?

Answer: Strong

PEPPA PIG

The answers are all characters from *Peppa Pig*, but the questions for older players are not about *Peppa Pig*.

YOUNGER: Who giggles, wears a turquoise dress and is a rabbit?

OLDER: Which Daphne du Maurier novel of 1938 is set in Cornwall?

Answer: Rebecca

YOUNGER: Who loves football and pirates, wears purple and is a dog?

OLDER: The 'Londonderry Air' has been given lyrics featuring what name?

Answer: Danny

YOUNGER: Who likes building blocks, wears yellow and is an elephant?

OLDER: Which was the middle Brontë sister?

Answer: Emily

SET 5 SCORECARD				
	Player 1	Player 2	Player 3	Player 4
Game 1				
Game 2				
Game 3				
Game 4				
Totals				

WINNER!

SET 6

... in which you will be tapping your toes in complete silence

GAME 1
CREDIT WHERE IT'S DUE

You need: noise-makers
Players: 2 or more plus someone to read out the questions
Scoring: 2 points for every correct answer

Before he was Jett in *Giant*, before he was Jim in *Rebel Without a Cause*, James Dean inhabited other roles for which he is less immediately remembered. Perhaps unfairly in the case of his turn in 1952's *Has Anybody Seen My Gal?*, where he embodies the (uncredited) role of Youth at Soda Fountain as surely no other performer could.

This game asks you to identify actors, starting with their less celebrated roles. Make a noise when you think you know the answer. You are *not* frozen out on a bad guess, so go nuts - just as nuts as Youth at Soda Fountain, whose soda includes malt, extra milk, extra chocolate and two dollops of ice cream, an order which would look ridiculous if given by anyone but Jimmy Dean.

ACTOR ONE

Dr Claire Lewicki

Grace Stewart

Gertrude Bell

Martha Gellhorn

Grace Kelly

Virginia Woolf

Answer: Nicole Kidman

ACTOR TWO

Robert Dudley, Earl of Leicester

Eames

Charles Bronson

Bane

Reginald Kray

Ronald Kray

Answer: Tom Hardy

ACTOR THREE

Sir Fopling Flutter

Lt Colonel William ('Bill') Tanner, MI5

Denis Thatcher

Craig Oliver

Lord Lucan

Prime Minister Michael Callow

Answer: Rory Kinnear

ACTOR FOUR

Blanche DuBois

Queen Elizabeth II

Queen Elizabeth I

Galadriel

Bob Dylan

Katharine Hepburn

Answer: Cate Blanchett

ACTOR FIVE

Dormouse

Goldie Locks

Daphne Honeybutt

Sadie Tomkins

Nurse Sandra

Nurse Susan Ball

Answer: Barbara Windsor

ACTOR SIX

Carol Thatcher

PC Doris Thatcher

Sally Owen

Sophie Chapman

Queen Elizabeth II

Queen Anne

Answer: Olivia Colman

GAME 2

WIN WHEN THEY'RE SINGING

You need: a phone each (and an extra one for the 'DJ')
Players: any number
Scoring: 2 points for whoever's nearest each time

Take it in turns to be the DJ. Everyone else gets up a stopwatch app.

When it's your turn, get up one of the songs below. Press play and then shout 'NOW' when the music starts,* and everyone else will press START.

After a few seconds, cut off the sound but let the song play on. Everyone else must now press STOP when they think the vocals begin.

Once everyone has pressed STOP, they will hold up their phones. Now you play the song again, and use a stopwatch on the other phone to give the actual answer. Whoever's closest gets the 2 points.

You can choose songs you think your group will know; we've had fun with these ones:

* There may be ads, or – worse – the official video might show the band faffing about before the music starts, or – worse again – a clown placing a needle on a gramophone record (extra point if you remember what song that is).

1. 'Stand By Me'
2. 'The Final Countdown'
3. 'Tragedy' (the Steps version, of course)
4. 'Somewhere Only We Know'
5. 'Papa Was a Rolling Stone'
6. 'Eye of the Tiger'
7. 'Clocks'
8. 'Common People'
9. 'Africa'
10. 'Shaft'

GAME 3
SIZE MATTERS #1

You need: pencil and paper for each player
Players: any number
Scoring: see below

In this game, we give you a category and everyone writes down something they think is in that category.

You get 2 points if you've written the longest correct answer of all the guesses (count letters but not spaces, punctuation, etc.).

And you get 4 points if you've managed to find the longest of all the possible answers. We've listed them in order of bigness.

GIFTS IN 'THE TWELVE DAYS OF CHRISTMAS'

(spell out the numbers: 'eleven', 'seven' and so on)

Twelve drummers drumming

A partridge in a pear tree

Seven swans a-swimming

Eight maids a-milking

Eleven pipers piping

Nine ladies dancing

Four calling birds

Ten lords a-leaping

Five golden rings

Six geese a-laying

Three French hens

Two turtle doves

(If your family uses a different version – that is, a wrong one – you are perfectly free to write that out and count the letters yourself.)

NATIVE TREES OF THE UK

The Woodland Trust of course defines a native tree as a species that has made its way to the UK naturally and that has recolonised the land when the glaciers melted after the last ice age and before the UK was disconnected from mainland Europe – but you know what we mean, you can't have a ylang ylang just because you once saw one in the Palm House at a botanical garden and wondered how to pronounce the name)

Purging Buckthorn
Wild Service Tree
Midland Hawthorn
Large Leaved Lime
Small Leaved Lime
Alder Buckthorn
Common Hawthorn
Plymouth Pear
Common Beech
Silver Birch
White Willow
Guelder Rose
Black Poplar
Crack Willow
Downy Birch
Osier Willow
Blackthorn
Bird Cherry
Common Lime
Field Maple
English Oak
Sessile Oak
Goat Willow
Grey Willow
Common Box
Bay Willow
Crab Apple
Scots Pine
Whitebeam
Hornbeam
Dogwood
Wych Elm
Spindle
Juniper
Alder
Aspen
Hazel
Holly
Rowan
Ash
Yew

LEADERS AT THE G7/G8 SUMMITS DURING THE 2010S

François Hollande
Stephen Harper
Enrico Letta
Silvio Berlusconi
Vladimir Putin
Matteo Renzi
Dmitry Medvedev
Yoshihiko Noda
Mario Monti
Emmanuel Macron
Angela Merkel
Theresa May
Nicolas Sarkozy
David Cameron
Shinzo Abe
Paolo Gentiloni
Barack Obama
Naoto Kan
Justin Trudeau
Donald Trump

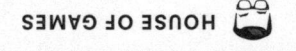

SPORTS AT THE 2020 OLYMPIC GAMES

(as in, not including separate athletic events)

Modern Pentathlon
Taekwondo
Sailing
Skateboarding
Triathlon
Surfing
Sport Climbing
Wrestling
Boxing
Weightlifting
Aquatics
Hockey
Table Tennis
Baseball
Karate
Basketball
Football
Rowing
Equestrian
Handball
Tennis
Gymnastics
Shooting
Canoe
Volleyball
Archery
Rugby
Athletics
Cycling
Golf
Badminton
Fencing
Judo

GAME 4

HIGHBROW LOWBROW – THE ORIGINAL GAME

You need: a coin
Players: 2 players or 2 teams
Scoring: 5 for every correct answer

RO: Ah, this one's a favourite of mine.

AC: You say that about all the games. Anyway, this time we're not going to play it like we do on the show, where there are two questions with the same answer.

RO: We're not?

AC: No. We're going to show the readers the *original* format of this game.

RO: Right, because the one we use works really well. That's why we use it.

AC: It does. But it can be tricky to write. We come up with a great highbrow question about Greek myths, but then you spend ages trying to find an *EastEnders* character called Terpsichore.

RO: Yeah, like you don't all watch all the soaps and reality shows. I mean, when you're not working on ***House of Games***, you're all on quizzes that are full of that stuff. Shows like–

AC: We agreed not to be publicly rude about that show. Or *that* one. Or *any* of the ones *he* hosts.

In this game, you flip a coin. Whoever calls the toss gets to choose either:

1) lowbrow questions about the periodic table, or

2) highbrow questions about the FIFA 100 top players.

Whichever you choose, you'll need to use both scholarly and pop-culture knowledge to get the points.

LOWBROW QUESTIONS ABOUT THE PERIODIC TABLE

Name these blockbuster movies from the tagline. Each movie has an element from the periodic table in its title.

26 **Fe** 55.845	Heroes aren't born. They're built.
50 **Sn** 118.710	Golf pro. Love amateur.
79 **Au** 196.967	A New Breed of Evil.

HIGHBROW QUESTIONS ABOUT FOOTBALLING GREATS

Which Brazilian FIFA 100 footballer shares a name with the man who said this?

‘ἓν οἶδα ὅτι οὐδὲν οἶδα’

(if you need it in English, ‘I know nothing except the fact of my ignorance’)

Which British FIFA 100 footballer’s surname completes this description of a suitor given by Portia in *The Merchant of Venice*?

> *‘Very vilely in the morning, when he is sober, and most vilely in the afternoon, when he is drunk: when he is ____, he is a little worse than a man’*

Which French FIFA 100 footballer shares his surname with the name of the king who said this?

> *‘An illiterate king is a crowned ass’*

Answers:
Periodic Table: *Iron Man*, *Tin Cup*, *Austin Powers in Goldmember*
FIFA 100: Sócrates, Best, Henry

SET 6 SCORECARD				
	Player 1	Player 2	Player 3	Player 4
Game 1				
Game 2				
Game 3				
Game 4				
Totals				

WINNER!

SET 7

… in which you'll discover which of you is the luckiest

GAME 1
FINGERS OFF BUZZERS #3

You need: a buzzer or other piece of noise-making equipment each
Players: any number, plus someone to read things out
Scoring: see below

The rules here are simple: every time you're the first to buzz with a correct answer, you get a point, *but* if the correct answer begins with the Letter of Doom, you lose all your points so far. That applies even if you don't give an answer; you only have to buzz to get the penalty.

Person reading out: we've put an asterisk next to the Letter of Doom answers, and given you a Richard Osman-style friendly introduction so that no one can complain that they don't understand what they've been asked to do. Keep up the pace to trick them into blurting out an answer.

'I'll say a word in French, you tell me what it means in English The Letter of Doom is ... L.'

avec (with)	*gauche* (left)*
je (I)	*notre* (our)
mais (but)	*plus* (more)
autre (other)	*moins* (less)*
lait (milk)	*cœur* (heart)
droit (right)	*premier* (first)

dernier (last)*

vert (green)

Edinbourg (Edinburgh)

Londres (London)*

huit (eight)

vache (cow)

peu (little)*

jeudi (Thursday)

août (August)

amour (love)*

GAME 2
UNLUCKY FOR SOME #1

You need: 4 things numbered 1–4; a bag
Players: 4 (take it in turns to ask questions or have a fifth player do that)
Scoring: 2 points for every correct answer

AC: Who would you say has been our unluckiest contestant?

RO: Katie Derham. No doubt about it.

AC: Mind you, she's never lucky. On *Strictly* she made it to the final but was first to be eliminated. On *Pointless Celebrities*, she went out on a question on her own area: classical music.

RO: To be fair that's because her partner ...

AC: ... the BBC arts editor ...

RO: ... the BBC arts editor had a brain-freeze and said 'Vivaldi' instead of 'Verdi'. And on *House of Games* she came second every single day. That's what happens when you're put up against Richard Herring, J.B. Gill and Rachel Riley. J.B.'s incredibly quick, we all know how Rachel Riley's brain works and Richard Herring is ... what's the word?

AC: ... 'tenacious'?

RO: Among other words.

In this game, you might be lucky, and you might not.

First, read out a question.

Then, each player draws a number from a bag (see above). Whoever draws '1' gets to guess first. Whoever draws '2' gets to guess second. You *must* be able to guess what happens to the other players.

Going first means you've definitely got a chance of getting those 2 points, but going later means a wrong option or two have already been eliminated ...

1. In the 2010 horror movie *Rubber*, residents of a town are terrorised by a sentient, telekinetic what?

   Tyre
   Eraser
   Toy duck
   Elastic band

2. Which regular *Carry On* actor wrote the lyrics to the Seekers' hit song 'Georgy Girl'?

   Jim Dale
   Hattie Jacques
   Kenneth Connor
   June Whitfield

3. Why did FIFA fine the FA 70,000 Swiss francs during the 2018 World Cup?

   Players missing press conferences
   Players wearing unauthorised socks
   Players arriving late to a stadium
   Players drinking non-sponsored beverages

4. Which of these is the title of a 1993 Guns N' Roses album?

The Lasagne Occurrence?
The Pasta Problem?
The Bolognese Dilemma?
The Spaghetti Incident?

(Yes, the question marks are intentional.)

5. Which actor's given middle name is Tiffany?

Kate Hudson
Richard Gere
Julia Roberts
Nicolas Cage

Answers: 1. Tyre (the tyre is called Robert) 2. Jim Dale 3. Three England players wore non-authorised socks over their official socks 4. *The Spaghetti Incident?* 5. Richard Gere (Kate's middle name is Garry, Julia's is Fiona and Nic's is Kim - yes, we call him Nic)

GAME 3

HIGHBROW LOWBROW - THE ACTUAL GAME #1

You need: your House of Games Spoiler Blocker
Players: 2 pairs
Scoring: see below

RO: You know we played the prototype Highbrow Lowbrow in Game 4 on page 93? Tell me we're going to give them the real–

AC: Right ahead of you, Skipper.

RO: I've asked you not to call me that.

When it's your pair's turn to answer, ask one of the other pair to read you a Highbrow Question. If you get it right, that's 5 points. If you don't, ask them to read the Lowbrow Question.

The answer is the same, but if you need both, you get only 1 point.

HIGHBROW: What term is used to refer to light and elegant English drawing-room furniture of the 1750s and 1760s made in a modified rococo style?

LOWBROW: What kind of performer wears a 'shirt' that's actually just a collar and cuffs?

Answer: Chippendale (NB Chippendales tried to trademark the collar-and-cuffs combo but it was deemed insufficiently distinctive - perhaps by Judge Snagglepuss?)

HIGHBROW: In a tragedy by Shakespeare, which dictator's words include the phrase 'Cry havoc and let slip the dogs of war!'?

LOWBROW: In *Carry on Cleo*, who is Kenneth Williams playing when he performs his infamous 'Infamy, infamy' line?

Answer: Julius Caesar

HIGHBROW: Napoleon's second abdication followed his decisive defeat at which battle of the Napoleonic Wars?

LOWBROW: Which song won Eurovision for Sweden in 1974?

Answer: Waterloo

HIGHBROW: What mock 'form' of Latin is produced by transferring the initial consonant of a word to its beginning and adding a vocalic syllable?

LOWBROW: What kind of animal was Rupert, who played the piano on *Britain's Got Talent*?

Answer: Pig ('Pig Latin' is a way of talking in code, so Richard Osman's *House of Games* becomes 'Ichard-ray Man-ozz-ay's Ouse-hay of Ames-gay')

HIGHBROW: Which film of 1987 is a retelling of Edmond Rostand's 1897 verse drama *Cyrano de Bergerac*?

LOWBROW: Which 1979 Police single was written in Paris's red-light district?

Answer: Roxanne

HIGHBROW: What nationality was Oscar Niemeyer, the modernist architect who worked on the United Nations Headquarters in New York?

LOWBROW: What kind of bum lift did *TOWIE*'s Lauren Goodger pay £10,000 for?

Answer: Brazilian (public-service announcement: listen up, readers – the Brazilian bum lift involves taking fat from elsewhere in the body and adding it to the bottom, so not everyone considers it the cleverest thing you could do to your bottom)

GAME 4

THE BACKWARDS ROUND

You need: buzzers or something else that makes a distinctive sound per player
Players: two or more, and someone to read the questions
Scoring: 2 points for every correct answer

AC: Idea funny really a had I've–

RO: Not let's.

If you're the one reading these backwards questions, enjoy it. You're *supposed* to sound silly. But you also get to be the one who corrects the others if they fail to give the answer backwards.

10. Product pastry based-meat which producing for famous is Mowbray Melton of town the?

9. *Wain Hay The* painted artist English which?

8. Gilbert Elizabeth by name same the of book a on based was, Roberts Julia starring, film 2010 which?

7. 2018 March of beginning the at UK the in arrived that system weather Siberian the for nickname the was what?

6. 'Bird Free' and 'Alabama Home Sweet' includes repertoire band's rock which?

5. **Tennis table of name original the was claim Johnson Boris did what Olympics 2012 the at?**

4. **City which on centred Staffordshire in region a is Potteries the?**

3. **Magicians criminal as Fisher Isla and Eisenberg Jesse starred film 2013 which?**

2. **Verne Jules by novel 1869 which in character a is Nemo Captain?**

1. **Act which by songs all: 'Dancing Be Should You', 'You to Message a Get Gotta I've', 'Love Your Is Deep How', '1941 Disaster Mining York New'?**

Answers: 10. Pie pork 9. Constable John 8. *Love Pray Eat* 7. East the from Beast (The) 6. Skynyrd Lynyrd 5. Whaff whiff 4. Trent-on-Stoke 3. *Me See You Now* 2. *Sea the Under Leagues Thousand Twenty* 1. Gees Bee (The)

SET 7 SCORECARD				
	Player 1	Player 2	Player 3	Player 4
Game 1				
Game 2				
Game 3				
Game 4				
Totals				

WINNER!

SET 8

... in which you will try to avoid ants

GAME 1
SIZE MATTERS #2

You need: pencil and paper for each player
Players: any number
Scoring: see below

In this game, we give you a category and everyone writes down something they think is in that category.

You get 2 points if you've written the longest correct answer of all the guesses (count letters but not spaces, punctuation, etc.).

And you get 4 points if you've managed to find the longest of all the possible answers. We've listed them in order of bigness.

WINNERS OF EUROVISION IN THE TWENTY-FIRST CENTURY

Azerbaijan
Portugal
Austria
Denmark
Estonia
Finland
Germany
Ukraine
Greece
Israel
Latvia
Norway
Russia
Serbia
Sweden
Turkey

BOOKS OF THE NEW TESTAMENT

(King James version, leave out any numbers)

Titus
Acts
John
Jude
Luke
Mark

Philemon
Hebrews
Matthew
Timothy
Romans
James
Peter

Thessalonians
Corinthians
Philippians
Colossians
Revelation
Ephesians
Galatians

THE CHRONICLES OF NARNIA

(not including any subtitles)

The Lion, the Witch and the Wardrobe
The Voyage of the Dawn Treader
The Magician's Nephew
The Horse and His Boy
The Silver Chair
Prince Caspian
The Last Battle

LANDLOCKED COUNTRIES

(those which are surrounded on all sides by other countries and do not have an ocean border)

Central African Republic
Czech Republic
Liechtenstein
Turkmenistan
Afghanistan
Burkina Faso
Switzerland
Azerbaijan
Kazakhstan
Kyrgyzstan
Luxembourg
South Sudan
Tajikistan
Uzbekistan
Macedonia

San Marino
Swaziland
Botswana
Ethiopia
Mongolia
Paraguay
Slovakia
West Bank
Zimbabwe
Andorra
Armenia
Austria
Belarus
Bolivia
Burundi

Hungary
Lesotho
Moldova
Bhutan
Kosovo
Malawi
Rwanda
Serbia
Uganda
Zambia
Nepal
Niger
Chad
Laos
Mali

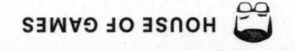

GAME 2

I PUT A SPELL ON YOU

You need: buzzers or something else that makes a distinctive sound per player

Players: pairs, plus someone to read the questions

Scoring: 2 points

You play in pairs. Choose wisely.

Buzz in when you think you know the answer. Then your partner must try to spell the answer. If both answer and spelling are correct, you get a point each.

If you're the one reading the questions, get them to do the spelling slowly and make some sort of positive or negative sound after each letter to really ramp up the tension.

1. What Philistine name for the devil is used in the lyrics to 'Bohemian Rhapsody'?

2. George Formby was known for playing something that combines a banjo with which other stringed instrument?

3. In the *Star Wars* films, what is the home planet of Anakin and Luke Skywalker?

4. Which clown from the *commedia dell'arte* tradition is invited to perform a fandango in the lyrics to 'Bohemian Rhapsody'?

5. **Literally meaning 'until we see each other again', what is the German for goodbye?**

6. **The first *Carry On* film, in which Bob Monkhouse is called up to join the army, is *Carry On* … what?**

7. **Which jukebox musical has a title that is also used in the lyrics to 'Bohemian Rhapsody'?**

8. **Which small genus of flowering bulbs has a name that rhymes with 'Freeman Hardy Willis'?**

9. **Which Pisan astronomer is referred to repeatedly in the lyrics to 'Bohemian Rhapsody'?**

10. **Talking of 'Bohemian Rhapsody', which 'poor boy', originally from the Arabian Nights stories, is the son of Widow Twankey?**

11. **What French word is used for a sachet of dried aromatic bark, petals and wood shavings?**

12. **Which Queen song is now getting its sixth mention in this game?**

Answers: 1. Beelzebub 2. Ukulele 3. Tatooine 4. Scaramouche 5. Auf Wiedersehen 6. Sergeant 7. *Mamma Mia!* (you can be lenient or not about the exclamation mark) 8. Amaryllis 9. Galileo (accept Galileo Galilei but that's just a contestant making things trickier for themselves in order to show off) 10. Aladdin 11. Potpourri 12. 'Bohemian Rhapsody'

GAME 3

THE ELEPHANT IN THE ROOM

You need: a noise-making device that each player can use as a buzzer

Players: 2 or more, plus someone to read out the clues

Scoring: 2 for every correct answer

If you're reading this at Christmas, you'll be well prepared for a game in which you have to avoid mentioning certain things. These include whatever the UK's relationship is with Europe by the time you read this, of course, but also hotter potatoes: what on earth went so badly wrong with Uncle Paul's dental surgery; the amount of time Grandma is spending in the loo; and the way that everybody left their bread sauce completely untouched after they spotted *that thing* in the sauce boat. Everybody except Grandma, that is.

The things to avoid in this game are much less stressful. For example, if the elephant in the room is the word BIN and the question is 'What's the Italian for baby?', you don't say 'bambino', you leave out the BIN and say 'bamo'.

Be gentle with each other about the pronunciations. Especially Uncle Paul.

ELEPHANT IN THE ROOM: ANT

1. What is the name of the continent where the South Pole is located?
2. Which Mexican-American guitarist had hits with 'Smooth' and 'Oye Como Va'?
3. What is the capital city of Chile?
4. In *Die Hard*, what rank is held by John McClane?
5. Which city in northern France is renowned for its lace and cream?
6. Which Cuban song lends its melody to terrace chants such as 'One team in Fulham / There's only one team in Fulham'?
7. What substance, similar to deodorant, is commonly put under the arms to reduce sweating?
8. Which duo has presented gameshows including *Friends Like These*, *PokerFace* and *Red or Black*?

ELEPHANT IN THE ROOM: EAR

1. The constellation Ursa Major is commonly known by what English name?
2. Which Vermeer painting shares its title with a 2003 period drama starring Scarlett Johansson?
3. What does the tax abbreviation PAYE stand for?

4. Which lawman is played by Burt Lancaster in *Gunfight at the O.K. Corral*?

5. Which US medal, first received in 1782, is an award for those wounded or killed in the service of their country?

6. As heard in the *Black Mirror* episode 'San Junipero', what is Belinda Carlisle's only UK number one to date?

7. Applause is technically forbidden in the House of Commons. What two-word phrase do MPs call out instead?

8. What animals are the Hanna-Barbera cartoon characters Boo Boo and Yogi?

Answers:

Ant
1. Arctica (accept the Arctic) 2. Carlos Sana 3. Siago 4. Detective Lieuten 5. Chilly 6. Guanamera 7. Iperspir 8. And Dec

Ear
1. (The) Great B 2. Girl with a Pl Ring 3. Pay As You N 4. Wyatt P 5. Purple Ht 6. Heaven Is a Place on Th 7. H H 8. Bs

GAME 4

FIVES ALIVES - GEOGRAPHY

You need: nothing
Players: any number
Scoring: no points - work together

RO: You'll find a few of these peppered throughout the book.

This one is Geography. You knew that from the title, I understand that. Anyway, here are some top fives, and the initial letters of the answers - but can you fill in those gaps?

A) THE WORLD'S MOST POPULOUS CITIES

1. S
2. B
3. K
4. I
5. D

B) THE HAPPIEST COUNTRIES IN THE WORLD

1. F
2. N
3. D
4. I
5. S

C) THE LEAST AFFORDABLE CITIES IN THE UK

1. O
2. L
3. W
4. C
5. C

D) WORLD CITIES WITH THE BUSIEST AIRPORTS

1. A
2. B
3. D
4. T
5. C

E) COUNTRIES WITH THE HIGHEST PERCENTAGE OF VEGETARIANS

1. I
2. I
3. I
4. A
5. G

Answers:

A) Shanghai, Beijing, Karachi, Istanbul, Dhaka (Source: *CEO* magazine)

B) Finland, Norway, Denmark, Iceland, Switzerland (Source: UN World Happiness Report)

C) Oxford, London, Winchester, Cambridge, Chichester (Source: Lloyds Bank report)

D) Atlanta, Beijing, Dubai, Tokyo, Chicago (Source: UN report)

E) India, Israel, Italy, Austria, Germany (Source: World Atlas; the UK is 7th!)

SET 8 SCORECARD				
	Player 1	Player 2	Player 3	Player 4
Game 1				
Game 2				
Game 3				
Game 4				
Totals				

WINNER!

SET 9

... in which you will discover more chickens than you ever dreamed could exist

GAME 1

AND THE ANSWER ISN'T #2

You need: a smartphone or tablet; your House of Games Spoiler Blocker

Players: ideally 4; you could make it work with 2 but it's probably not worth it

Scoring: see below

These four questions are multiple-choice, but we haven't bothered to come up with the wrong ones. That's your job.

When it's your turn, everyone else looks at the question and its answer. Then (so that handwriting is no clue), someone takes the phone and types in (in random order) the right answer and a multi-choice option from each of the other players. (You shouldn't also type in any of the fun facts we offer as explanation.)

Then you get the phone, someone reads you the question, and you consider the options.

If you're right, you get a point. Obviously. But if you're wrong, the point goes to whoever invented the option you chose. Take your time ...

1. **What was the name of the Bank of America before it took on its current name in 1930?**

   Answer: The Bank of Italy (it was opened by Amadeo Peter Giannini in 1904)

2. **In 2017, what was the most requested specialist subject by contestants applying to be on the quiz show *Mastermind*?**

   Answer: Harry Potter (262 contestants wanted a quidditchy quiz)

3. **Before he decided on *Catch-22*, what title did Joseph Heller propose for his iconic novel?**

   Answer: Catch-18

4. **What seven-word phrase is believed to make up the last words of Elvis Presley?**

   Answer: 'I'm going to the bathroom to read'

GAME 2

TRY NOT TO GET ALL PHILOSOPHICAL

You need: a phone, tablet or computer each
Players: any number
Scoring: 2 points every time you win

RO: Are you sure this works?

AC: Do you want the ontological answer or the empirical one?

RO: I want the one where you tell me that you've tested it.

AC: I've tested it. The only way it could go wrong – that I can think of – is if someone decided to, say, edit the Richard Osman Wikipedia entry so that it began 'Richard Osman is a Richard Osman …' But I can't think of any reason why anyone would do that.

RO: Other than your having just suggested it?

AC: Ah.

Each player gets up a Wikipedia page for anything they like.

When everyone is ready, a nominated player calls out 'TAP!' and each player clicks or taps on the first link in the main article.

(This means that you ignore boxes about disambiguation, stuff in

brackets or italics, warnings that say 'This page has been locked because of an edit war among furious Pokémon fans', etc. The first proper link.)

Then whoever said 'TAP!' says 'TAP!' again, and everyone repeats the process.

If the page that comes up on your device is Philosophy, you call out 'Philosophy!' and leave the game. The same goes for Maths.

The last surviving player scoops up the 2 points.

And then you play again.

GAME 3

OPPOSITES ATTRACT

You need: nothing
Players: any number, take it in turns to read the clues
Scoring: 1 point for every correct answer

AC: What would you say is the most 'controversial' game in our harmless little show?

RO: Opposites Attract, without a doubt. Most people love it, but it makes some viewers absolutely irate. 'FOX ISNT THE OPOSSITE OF CHICKEN YOU IDOITS [*sic*]', that kind of thing.

AC: We're talking Twitter, aren't we?

RO: We are. It's a daft thing, really, Twitter. That's why I've been spending less time on it.

AC: Maybe we would have avoided all of this if we hadn't used the word 'opposite' and had called the game, like, Sandi Toksvig's Garden of Work, right? Richard?

RO: Hm?

AC: When you say you're 'spending less time' on Twitter ... are you live-tweeting this conversation?

RO: Already got a like from Sandi.

One person reads out a category and then some clues. The clues are *the least helpful ones we could think of.* So if the category was London Underground and the clue was 'Southern Circle', you would say 'Northern Line' for the point.

SHAKESPEARE PLAYS

1. The Miserable Husbands of Slough
2. Megacity
3. The Customer of Milan
4. Hate's Conservative's Found
5. The Gentle Breeze

Answers: 1. *The Merry Wives of Windsor* 2. *Hamlet* 3. *The Merchant of Venice* 4. *Love's Labour's Lost* 5. *The Tempest*

ANDREW LLOYD WEBBER MUSICALS

1. Satan Z-Lister
2. Moonrise Cul-de-sac
3. Hate Always Lives
4. Juan
5. Mary and the Rubbish Black and White Nightmare-trousers

Answers: 1. *Jesus Christ Superstar* 2. *Sunset Boulevard* 3. *Love Never Dies* 4. *Evita* 5. *Joseph and the Amazing Technicolor Dreamcoat*

COMPONENTS OF A CAR

1. Let go
2. Ballet shoe
3. Six-pack
4. Wood-burning stove
5. *Financial Times*

Answers: 1. Clutch 2. Boot 3. Spare tyre 4. Radiator 5. Mirror

CHARACTERS IN *THE SIMPSONS*

1. Mr Carpet-Sweeper
2. Mrs Salves
3. Napoleon
4. Aesop
5. The Tooth Fairy's Enormous Impediment

Answers: 1. Miss Hoover 2. Mr Burns 3. Nelson 4. Homer 5. Santa's Little Helper

GAME 4
CHICKENS OR DICKENS?

You need: nothing
Players: 2 or more, plus someone to read out the names
Scoring: 1 point for every correct answer

This game could not be simpler. One of you reads out the names below. The others take it in turns to say whether each is a kind of chicken, a character from Dickens, or both.

1. Leghorn: chicken
2. Silkie: chicken
3. Podsnap: pompous ass from *Our Mutual Friend*
4. Drummle: brute in *Great Expectations*
5. Marans: chicken
6. Welsummer: chicken
7. Buckeye: chicken
8. Wickfield: the real heroine of *David Copperfield*

9. Bantam: *both* a small chicken *and* a Master of Ceremonies in *The Pickwick Papers*
10. Australorp: chicken
11. Bazzard: clerk in *The Mystery of Edwin Drood*
12. Cruncher: porter in *A Tale of Two Cities*
13. Barnevelder: chicken
14. Cuttle: sea captain in *Dombey and Son*
15. Honeythunder: overblown oaf in *The Mystery of Edwin Drood*

SET 9 SCORECARD				
	Player 1	Player 2	Player 3	Player 4
Game 1				
Game 2				
Game 3				
Game 4				
Totals				

WINNER!

SET 10

... in which you will discover more Richards than you ever dreamed could exist

GAME 1
KING OF THE JUMBLE

You need: your House of Games Spoiler Blocker
Players: any number
Scoring: 2 points for every correct pair

Take it in turns to read a pair of clues to the person to your right.

They must give both answers, and the answers must have the same letters (though not in the same order; for that, you want Game 4, Page 93: Highbrow Lowbrow, or Game 4, Page 77: Generation vs Generation).

If they don't get both, play passes to the right.

1.

Gary from *SpongeBob SquarePants* or Brian from *The Magic Roundabout*

Cause of the stigmata in a grisly bit of the Easter story

Answer: Snail, Nails

2.

Country with Nikolai Tesla airport

Disease afflicting the dog in *To Kill a Mockingbird*

Answer: Serbia, Rabies

3.

Standard unit of electric charge

LA police series starring Peter Falk

Answer: Coulomb, Columbo

4.

Florid Puccini opera of 1900

Sporting venue six miles from Windsor Castle

Answer: *Tosca*, Ascot

5.

Government meeting called during a national emergency

Chocolate alternative said to have been eaten by John the Baptist

Answer: Cobra, Carob

6.

Voice of Po in *Kung Fu Panda*

Card game also known as Twenty-One

Answer: Jack Black, Blackjack

7.

Action that starts an arm-wrestling contest

Skull skin

Answer: Clasp, Scalp

8.

Pink substance flowing underground in *Ghostbusters II*

Units of distance preferred by the Proclaimers

Answer: Slime, Miles

9.

Scientist who was offered presidency of Israel

Decade during which Richard Osman appeared in *Drop the Dead Donkey*

Answer: Einstein, Nineties

10.

What Graham Norton does

Sadly missed pursuer of crocodiles

Answer: Interviews, Steve Irwin

GAME 2
EMOJI STORIES

You need: your House of Games Spoiler Blocker
Players: any number
Scoring: 2 points for every correct answer

RO: With this game, grown-ups should know that children have a good chance of knowing the answer, so it might be nice to let them puzzle things out. Assuming, that is, you're the kind of person who watches TV quizzes with your kids and yells out the answers to the ones that your kids could have got if you'd just kept quiet and let them have a little moment of pride.

AC: Are you talking to the readers, or to me?

RO: Which do you think?

AC: It's the only way they'll learn.

Use your House of Games Spoiler Blocker to reveal one set of emojis at a time. Each one represents a children's book. Two points for the first person to call out the title each time. *Bonus point* if you can follow up with the author's name, too.

1. 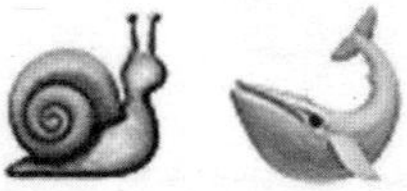

2. 

3. 

4. 

5. 

6. 

7. 

8. 

9. 

10. 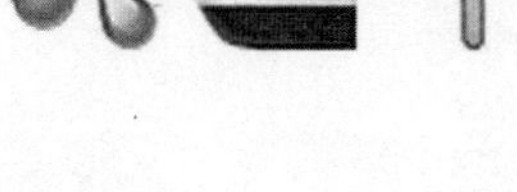

Answers:

1. *The Snail and the Whale*
Julia Donaldson & Axel Scheffler

2. *Charlie and the Chocolate Factory*
Roald Dahl

3. *The Silver Chair*
C.S. Lewis

4. *The Sheep-Pig*
Dick King-Smith

5. *The Curious Incident of the Dog in the Night-Time*
Mark Haddon

6. *Noughts & Crosses*
Malorie Blackman

7. *Alice through the Looking-Glass* (officially titled *Through the Looking-Glass, and What Alice Found There*)
Lewis Carroll

8. *Tintin in America*
Hergé

9. *Five Go Off to Camp* (but take a point if you've said any Famous Five title, they're basically all the same)
Enid Blyton

10. *Watership Down*
Richard Adams

GAME 3

WHICH RICH IS WHICH?

You need: buzzers or other noise-makers
Players: 3 or more
Scoring: 2 points for every correct answer

RO: How did we come up with this again? I'm pretty sure we–

AC: –started with the name, that's right.

In this game, every answer is *a different single forename*, each a variant of the name Richard.

One player acts as the reader of the questions. If this is you, have fun with it. Read them nice and slowly. After all, the others already have a pretty good idea of what the first name might be. Because of that, the first clue should often be enough, if you leave a pause. If not, leave an especially dramatic pause after saying 'Surname' and read the surname itself out as slowly as you think you can get away with.

1.

Shot an attorney during a quail hunt

Played onscreen by Richard Dreyfuss and Christian Bale

Surname ... Cheney

Answer: Dick

2.

Winner, second-ever week of *House of Games*

Presenter of TV show *River Hunters* (by the time this book is published, all being well)

Surname ... Edwards

Answer: Rick*

3.

Created fictional country-music star Otis Lee Crenshaw

Always described as 'gravel-voiced'

Surname ... Hall

Answer: Rich

4.

Began career aged 12 as member of *[do a Puerto Rican accent]* Menudo

Biggest hit celebrates a 'crazy life' in Spanish language

Surname ... Martin

Answer: Ricky

* This Rick was also in the *House of Games* pilot, so although he was the winner of series 1, week 2, you could argue that he was always at something of an advantage.

5.

Played club cricket alongside Michael Parkinson

Officiated more test matches than anyone before

Surname … Bird

Answer: Dicky

6.

Spent the 2010–11 season without a shirt number

Scored winning goal against England in 2004 despite being goalkeeper

Surname (not that it's as relevant this time) … Pereira

Answer: Ricardo

7.

Shares first name and surname with trombonist in the Specials

Plays Manny in *Modern Family*

Surname … Rodriguez

Answer: Rico

8.

Buried in March 2015 with a reading from relative Benedict Cumberbatch

Suspected of having his nephews killed

Surname … let's say Plantagenet

Answer: Richard (III)

9.

Middle name is a dollar sign

Young comics trillionaire

Surname ... Rich

Answer: Richie

10.

And finally, something different:

Even if you haven't seen *A Man for All Seasons*, you should be able to guess this man's name. Keep calling out your guesses until someone gives the name below. First, here is a portrait of him by Hans Holbein the Younger.

This man was a speaker of the House of Commons and Lord Chancellor. He loved overseeing the torture of bishops in the Tower of London and sometimes turned the wheels on the rack with his own hands. After helping execute the will of Henry VIII, he was made a member of the nobility, and we are looking for his title as part of the answer. His rank was the one which comes after duke, marquess, earl and viscount, and he was the initial holder of the title. Keep guessing ...

Answer: Richard Rich, (the) 1st Baron Rich

GAME 4
BOOK GAMES OF OSMAN RICHARD'S

You need: buzzers, or noise-makers of some stripe
Players: 2 or more, plus someone to read the questions
Scoring: 2 points for every correct answer

RO: Ah, this is the one where the words come backwards.

AC: No, that's what I always think, but that's The Backwards Round (Game 4, Page 108).*

RO: Yes, you're right. OK. So this is the one where the Zs, Ys and Xs appear first and finally the Cs, Bs and As.

AC: Yes! No, wait. That's Z to A.

RO: You're right. And we've already done that. Haven't we?

AC: Yes. Wait, no. BBC Books said that that isn't how paper works, remember?

RO: Yes, you're right. It's the one where we give the words of the question in alphabetical order.

AC: We don't have a game like that. Yet.

RO: Shall we just play the thing?

---

* This is pretty much verbatim about a hundred conversations in the *House of Games* office.

'I'm sorry: if you buzz you *must* answer!'

If you're the one asking the questions, feel free to borrow Jeremy Paxman's stentorian catchphrase. Because here, players give the answer with the words rearranged in *alphabetical order.* In fact, feel free to remove points from anyone who doesn't answer immediately.

1. What is bingo-callers' slang for the number 88?
2. In texting, what does the abbreviation 'TMI' stand for?
3. Who is the feline mascot of Frosties?
4. In poker, what is the name for a hand that consists a triplet of cards of the same rank?
5. What were the first six words spoken by Neil Armstrong when he stepped on to the Moon?
6. In the King James Bible, what is the sixth commandment? Keep guessing ...
7. What is the three-part name of the character, created in 1928 by Joyce Lankester Brisley, who wears a pink and white striped dress?
8. What is the famous first line of the novel *Moby Dick*?
9. What two-word nickname does Christopher Robin give to his honey-loving friend from the Hundred Acre Wood?
10. Which of Shakespeare's comedies has a title that means 'a big fuss over not a lot'?

Answers: 1. Fat Ladies Two 2. Information Much Too 3. the tiger tony 4. A kind of three 5. For man one small step that's 6. Kill Not Shalt Thou 7. Mandy-Milly-Molly 8. Call Ishmael me 9. Bear pooh 10. About Ado Much Nothing

SET 10 SCORECARD				
	Player 1	Player 2	Player 3	Player 4
Game 1				
Game 2				
Game 3				
Game 4				
Totals				

WINNER!

SET 11

... in which you will see colours that aren't really there

GAME 1
I'M TERRIBLE AT DATING

You need: pencil and paper, a phone with calculator, your House of Games Spoiler Blocker

Players: 2 or more

Scoring: 2 points for whoever is closest each time

RO: What's the worst answer you've ever given to one of these? Be honest.

AC: I was literally centuries out on the date of Attila the Hun's sacking of Italy.

RO: 'Literally centuries'? Come back to me when you measure your mistakes in larger units.

AC: Ah, yes. When was it you said the Taj Mahal was built?

RO: Literally a millennium before it was.*

For every event below, write down your guess when it took place. Use your House of Games Spoiler Blocker to block off each time.

It's as simple as that.

---

* This is also all true. We all do atrociously at some of these Dating questions, happy in the knowledge our ignorance will not be broadcast to an adoring teatime TV audience.

Except it's not simple, because you're going to be embarrassingly wrong on some of them. We'll start with a couple of easy ones.

1. **Abraham Lincoln is assassinated**

   Answer: 1865

2. **Geoffrey Chaucer dies**

   Answer: 1400

3. **Richard Strauss composes his retrospective piece *Vier letzte Lieder***

   Answer: 1948 (Richard Strauss is not related to the nineteenth-century waltzing Strausses)

4. **A monarch of England succeeds his or her grandparent for the last time (as we type this now)**

   Answer: 1760 (George III took the reins from George II)

5. **First untethered human flight in a hot-air balloon**

   Answer: 1783

6. **The first Rugby World Cup is played**

   Answer: 1987

7. **Isaac Newton publishes his laws of motion**

   Answer: 1687

8. **Confucius is born**

   Answer: 551 BC

9. **Dinosaurs are made extinct (estimate necessarily rounded to the nearest million years)**

Answer: 66,000,000 BC

10. **Tchaikovsky's 1812 Overture is first performed***

Answer: 1882

* It's sometimes still performed with real cannons!**

** Alright, 'real cannon', if you insist.***

*** Okay, 'all right', if you're that kind of pedant.****

**** Very well, 'OK', if you want to be that guy.*****

***** Yes, or 'that girl', fair enough.

GAME 2

HIGHBROW LOWBROW – THE ACTUAL GAME #2

You need: your House of Games Spoiler Blocker
Players: 2 pairs
Scoring: see below

When it's your pair's turn to answer, ask one of the other pair to read you one of the Highbrow Questions. If you get it right, that's 5 points. If you don't, ask them to read the Lowbrow Question.

The answer is the same, but if you need both, you get only 1 point.

By the way, the Lowbrow Questions aren't necessarily easier. So why are they worth less? It's because we know that you're embarrassed about the fact that you could probably recite the dialogue to *One Fine Day* from memory. We don't think you *should* feel guilty – especially the puddle scene – but we are happy to turn that embarrassment into a game.

HIGHBROW: Which 'burlesque in song and dance' by Stravinsky takes its one-word title from the French for 'fox'?

LOWBROW: Which Bond baddie, also known as Victor Zokas, is played by a shaven-headed Robert Carlyle?

Answer: Renard

HIGHBROW: In 1993, Toni Morrison was awarded the Nobel Prize for Literature, following the publication of which of her novels?

LOWBROW: What's Utah's basketball team called?

Answer: Jazz

HIGHBROW: In typesetting, what name is given to a distracting line of white space which accidentally appears between the words?

LOWBROW: In Texas Hold 'Em poker, what's the last card dealt called?

Answer: River

HIGHBROW: What familiar name is common to the kings George VI and Edward VII, and the Taoiseach of Ireland from 1997 to 2008?

LOWBROW: What's Burnley's bee mascot called?

Answer: Bertie (both monarchs were named Albert, Bertie in the family; Patrick Bartholomew Ahern is also known as Bertie)

HIGHBROW: Of what nickname did the US president of 1901–9 say, 'if it is used by anyone it is a sure sign he does not know me'?

LOWBROW: What item of lingerie, once called the camiknicker, was worn by Cybill Shepherd in *Moonlighting* and enjoyed a surge in popularity in the 1980s?

Answer: Teddy

HIGHBROW: Which native American tribe, known as the Keepers of the Eastern Door, fought alongside the British in the War of Independence?

LOWBROW: What hairdo did Alex Ferguson make David Beckham remove before the Charity Shield match in the year 2000?

Answer: Mohawk (NB you may or may not want to give a point for 'Mohican', but bear in mind: (a) the Mohicans are a different tribe, who fought the Mohawk; (b) a mohican hairdo sticks up while a mohawk is a line of brush.) Incidentally, Beckham hid his new do under a hat, which he only took off at the last minute. When told to remove it, Beckham recalls, 'I said no at first and then I saw his face change very quickly so I went and shaved it off in the toilet. He was very strict.'

GAME 3
DIM SUMS

You need: nothing
Players: any number, ideally 4
Scoring: 5 for every correct answer

Two heads are better than one in this game, so ideally you'll be playing in pairs.

And those pairs should take turns to look at the questions below. Each one has an incomplete sum, and four statements. Each statement describes a number, and your job is to choose which of the statements completes the empty sum.

CHRISTMAS

_____ ÷ _____ = 333

Year that the Spice Girls had a Christmas number one with 'Goodbye'

Number of geese-a-laying in the lyrics to 'The Twelve Days of Christmas'

Year that the Spice Girls had a Christmas number one with '2 Become 1'

Number of ghosts who visit in *A Christmas Carol* by Charles Dickens

WINSTON CHURCHILL

____ + ____ = 130

Last two digits of the year in which he became prime minister for the first time

His age in years when he died

Last two digits of the year in which he became prime minister for the second time

Length of time, in years, that he was married to Clementine

PURPLE

____ + ____ = 31

Number of Oscar nominations for Woody Allen's *The Purple Rose of Cairo*

Number of Oscar nominations for Steven Spielberg's *The Color Purple*

Highest number reached in the charts by Jimi Hendrix's 'Purple Haze'

Highest number reached in the charts by Deep Purple's 'Smoke on the Water'

UNITED ARAB EMIRATES

_____ - _____ = 1

Number of countries it borders

Number of emirates it contains

Number of buildings with more than 100 floors

Number of UNESCO World Heritage sites

Answers:

Christmas: Goodbye ÷ Geese
Year that the Spice Girls had a Christmas number one with 'Goodbye': 1998
Number of geese-a-laying in the lyrics to 'The Twelve Days of Christmas': 6
Year that the Spice Girls had a Christmas number one with '2 Become 1': 1996
Number of ghosts who visit in *A Christmas Carol* by Charles Dickens: 4

Winston Churchill: first time + died (or vice versa)
Last two digits of the year in which he became prime minister for the first time: 40
His age in years when he died: 90
Last two digits of the year in which he became prime minister for the second time: 51
Length of time, in years, that he was married to Clementine: 56

Purple: Color + Smoke (or vice versa)
Number of Oscar nominations for Woody Allen's *The Purple Rose of Cairo*: 1
Number of Oscar nominations for Steven Spielberg's *The Color Purple*: 10
Highest number reached in the charts by Jimi Hendrix's 'Purple Haze': 3
Highest number reached in the charts by Deep Purple's 'Smoke on the Water': 21

United Arab Emirates: Borders - UNESCO
Number of countries it borders: 2
Number of emirates it contains: 7
Number of buildings with more than 100 floors: 3
Number of UNESCO World Heritage sites: 1

GAME 4

THE ~~ALL-COLOUR~~ GREY FLAGS QUIZ

You need: nothing
Players: any number
Scoring: 2 points for every correct answer

AC: Vexillologists–

RO: I'm going to stop you already.

AC: Flag fans–

RO: That's better.

AC: Flag fans were pretty sad in 2011 when Libya re-adopted the stripy design they used in the old days. It meant that we lost the only national flag with only one colour!

RO: Yeah, listen–

AC: The good news for *Jamaica*, of course–

RO: Alan?

AC: What?

RO: Since we're talking about flags and colours. We *did* check that this book's pictures are going to be in colour, didn't we?

AC: Uh, I'm just going to have a quick tinker with our flag round. We'll talk about the Jamaican flag later, yeah?

RO: Take your time.

Take it in turns to answer the vexillological* questions below.

Some easy ones to start with ...

1. **If**  **is the German flag, whose flag is**  **?**

2. **If**  **is the Indian flag, whose flag is**  **?**

3. **If**  **is the French flag, whose flag is**  **?**

Taking it up a notch ...

4. **If**  **is the Scottish flag, whose flag is**  **?**

5. **If** 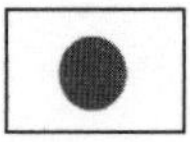 **is the Japanese flag, whose flag is**  **?**

6. **If**  **is the Icelandic flag, whose flag is**  **?**

7. **If**  **is the Swiss flag, whose flag is**  **?**

* If you are actually a vexillologist, in this grayscale quiz, treat all reds as the same red, likewise all blues, etc.

And some tougher ones ...

8. If  is the Italian flag, whose flag is  ?

9. If  is the Senegalese flag, whose flag is  ?

10. If  is the Romanian flag, whose flag is  ?

Answers: 1. Belgium 2. Ireland 3. Russia 4. Greece 5. Austria 6. Norway 7. Poland 8. Bulgaria 9. Mali (pretty much the same, only without the star) 10. Chad (weirdly nigh-on indistinguishable)

SET 11 SCORECARD				
	Player 1	Player 2	Player 3	Player 4
Game 1				
Game 2				
Game 3				
Game 4				
Totals				

WINNER!

SET 12

… in which we will receive letters of complaint from Tynesiders

GAME 1
CORRECTION CENTRE #1

You need: buzzers, or noise-makers of some sort
Players: any number, plus someone to read out the nonsense
Scoring: 2 for every correct answer

Take it in turns to read these statements aloud. Each of them is completely untrue. Buzz in when you know how changing *just one word* in the sentence will make it accurate.

1. **There is an exhibition dedicated to the Chuckle Brothers at the Smithsonian National Air & Space Museum.**

2. **In 1642, King Charles attempted to have MPs arrested – an action that led directly to intergalactic war.**

3. **In a varied career, Noël Coward wrote 5 short-story collections, 281 songs and 27 plays, many of them centred on drawing pins.**

4. **The lead characters in the 1988 horror film *Dead Ringers* are twins, both played by Rotary Irons.**

5. **The ontological argument for the existence of God was challenged by Brian Kant.**

6. **As a mark of respect, during the state funeral of Winston Churchill, a 90-gun salute was fired, and Big Brother went completely silent .**

7. **When New Year's Eve begins in New Zealand, it is still New Year's Eve in the UK.**

8. **In 2018, Theresa May presented Chinese premier Xi Jinping with a DVD box set of *Blue Peter*.**

9. **Often seen as an allegorical investigation of humanity's quest for wisdom and enlightenment, and heavy on Masonic imagery, *The Magic Roundabout* achieved immediate success on its premiere in 1791.**

10. **First sighted in 1775 and still one of the least hospitable places on earth, South Shields is home to elephant seals, king penguins and even a few hardy humans.**

Answers:

1. There is an exhibition dedicated to the **Wright** Brothers at the Smithsonian National Air & Space Museum
2. In 1642, King Charles attempted to have MPs arrested – an action that led directly to **civil war**.
3. In a varied career, Noël Coward wrote 5 short-story collections, 281 songs and 27 plays, many of them centred on drawing **rooms**.
4. The lead characters in the 1988 horror film *Dead Ringers* are twins, both played by **Jeremy** Irons.
5. The ontological argument for the existence of God was challenged by **Immanuel** Kant.
6. As a mark of respect, during the state funeral of Winston Churchill, a 90-gun salute was fired, and Big **Ben** went completely silent. (We are aware that this name, which everyone always uses, is not the official one.)
7. When New Year's **Day** begins in New Zealand, it is still New Year's Eve in the UK.
8. In 2018, Theresa May presented Chinese premier Xi Jinping with a DVD box set of *Blue **Planet***.
9. Often seen as an allegorical investigation of humanity's quest for wisdom and enlightenment, and heavy on Masonic imagery, *The Magic **Flute*** achieved immediate success on its premiere in 1791.
10. First sighted in 1775 and still one of the least hospital places on earth, South **Georgia** is home to elephant seals, king penguins and even a few hardy humans.

GAME 2
IT IS BRAIN SURGERY

You need: nothing
Players: someone to read from this book
Scoring: 4 points for every correct answer

RO: I get the feeling we ...

AC: ... started with the name again, that's right.

Hand the book over straightaway to someone who will be doing the reading.

Hello, someone who will be doing the reading. Read the following aloud, letting the details sink in. (Except for the part that starts 'Don't read this bit'.)

'This is a memory quiz. One player reads out the following passage, then asks the questions.'

Don't read this bit: you will be scratching yourself in five different places as you read.

'The first British neurosurgeon, and the first person to remove a spinal tumour, was Sir Victor Horsley [scratch your nose]. ***Sir Victor loved the thyroid glands of monkeys almost as much as he hated rabies but is best remembered today for developing the operative methods which allowed him to perform dozens of operations on human brains, 44 of which were successful.***

'More pioneering work was done by Scottish surgeon Sir William Macewen [scratch your head]. *In 1876, he showed that watching a patient's movements could reveal the location of abscesses in the brain. He had a chance to demonstrate this on a patient, but the family thought the surgery was too dangerous. It was not as dangerous as the abscess, which promptly killed the patient.*

'Other early surgeons worthy of note include Rickman Godlee [scratch your earlobe], *whose obituary in* The Times *described him as 'rather sarcastic', Hermann Schloffer* [scratch your side], *who gave his name to a tumour, and Harvey Cushing* [scratch your bottom], *who collected his findings in 1932 in the snappily titled "The Basophil Adenomas of the Pituitary Body and Their Clinical Manifestations: Pituitary Basophilism".*

'OK, that's the end of the text. Now, here comes the memory test. Shout when you know the answer.

'1 Sir Victor Horsley: when I first mentioned his name, where was I scratching myself? [nose]

'2 And Sir William Macewen. When I mentioned his name, I was also scratching myself. Where was I scratching this time? [head]

'3 Rickman Godlee. Where was the scratch? [earlobe]

'4 And for Hermann Schloffer? [side]

'5 Finally, Harvey Cushing? [bottom]

'OK, the points are [say who shouted what first]. *Thank you for playing, and I hope we've all learned something.'*

Well done, Reader. You did great.

GAME 3
QUESTION WRITERS' DAY OFF

You need: buzzers, or the willingness to make animal noises instead
Players: someone to read from this book
Scoring: 2 points for every correct answer

AC: Have you ever been to the *QI* offices?

RO: Gorgeous, aren't they? Light, airy, books everywhere. Bit like the old *Fifteen to One* HQ. Why do you ask?

AC: No reason. It's just ... well, it must be nice to see daylight every now and then.

RO: Tell you what: why don't you all leave your bunker and go home early?

AC: Aw, Richard. That's lovely.

RO: We'll still need some questions, of course.

These questions have been written by the children of the *House of Games* team. Buzz in (or make the noise of some other animal) when you think you know the answer. If you are wrong, you will not be frozen out. You'll see why: some of them might require multiple guesses. Thank you very much to Dulcie, Sol, Tommy, Nola and Raphael.

1. What is Ulan Bator the capital of?

2. On what show do they sometimes get children in or famous people, and the presenters do lots of challenges?

3. Do you know how big a T-Rex's eye is?

4. What Go Jetter has an X in their name?

5. What dwarf planet is after Pluto?

6. Do you know who my best friend is?

7. What did the Stuarts put in pudding?

8. Does Anthony like bananas?

9. Sophie's mum has four children. Their names are April, May and June. What's the other one?

10. What's more boring than school, even?

Answers: 1. Mongolia 2. *Blue Peter* 3. It's as big as an adult human fist! 4. Xuli 5. Haumea 6. Mummy, and sometimes Daddy 7. Flowers! 8. No, he doesn't like bananas 9. Sophie! 10. Daddy and his job

GAME 4
AND THE ANSWER ISN'T #3

You need: a smartphone or tablet; your House of Games Spoiler Blocker

Players: ideally 4; you could make it work with 2 but it's probably not worth it

Scoring: see below

These four questions are multiple-choice, but we haven't bothered to come up with the wrong ones. That's your job.

When it's your turn, everyone else looks at the question and its answer. Then (so that handwriting is no clue), someone takes the phone and types in (in random order) the right answer and a multi-choice option from each of the other players. (You shouldn't also type in any of the fun facts we offer as explanation.)

Then you get the phone, someone reads you the question, and you consider the options.

If you're right, you get a point. Obviously. But if you're wrong, the point goes to whoever invented the option you chose. Take your time ...

1. **By what name is the much loved children's book character Mr Bump known in Norway?**

   Answer: Herr Dumpidump

2. **Which major organisation has the motto Blood and Fire?**

   Answer: The Salvation Army (in reference to the blood of Christ and the fire of the Holy Spirit)

3. **In the years following 1952, a number of Scottish post-boxes were destroyed in protest against what?**

   Answer: Because they had the letters 'E II R' on them (the vandals insisted that the new queen should be known as Elizabeth I in Scotland; one post-box was blown up; the folk songs 'Sky High Joe' and 'The Ballad of the Inch' celebrate the acts)

4. **What's the meaning of the name of Namibia, the African country?**

   Answer: 'Area where there is nothing'

SET 12 SCORECARD				
	Player 1	Player 2	Player 3	Player 4
Game 1				
Game 2				
Game 3				
Game 4				
Totals				

WINNER!

SET 13

… in which a certain penguin might prove very useful

GAME 1
ALL IN THE DETAILS #1

You need: possibly pencil and paper; your House of Games Spoiler Blocker
Players: 2 or more
Scoring: see below

RO: Any advice for the people at home when it comes to All in the Details, Alan?

AC: Yes! If you're guessing, let your mind wander. One time we played this, Rachel Riley gave these clues to a novel –

The main characters are ... 'females olden times'
The first volume was published in ... 'normal-sized print'
It was written by ... 'maybe a feminist'

– which was still enough for Katie Derham to identify *Little Women*. This was the same episode where J.B. Gill had a complete brain-freeze and gave these clues to another novel –

It's set in ... 'a farm'
The plot involves ... 'animals'
It was written by ... 'George Orwell'

– which was *not* enough for Richard Herring to identify *Nineteen Eighty-Four.*

RO: That kind of thing can happen easily in a TV studio when you're playing game after game.

AC: Absolutely regrettable, those embarrassing moments.

RO: Yep. Hate them.

Take it in turns to reveal one of the Detail Sets below. If you want to keep this book pristine, write out the details on a piece of paper. Fill in the gaps with a few words. If you don't know the precise information - well, that's part of the fun. Put your best guess. (But don't put any of the words of the answer.)

Now, read out your completed Detail Set to the other players. Once you get to the end, everyone has as many guesses as they like. (Take it in turns or shout out depending how rambunctious you're feeling.)

If a player gets it right, they get a point - and so do you.

(By the way, we've also given what might have been the most useful answers - see below, but if you peek, you're missing the point of this game and, to be honest, games in general.)

1. LANDMARK

   It was opened in ...

   It's located in ...

   One of its distinguishing features is a ...

   Answer: Millennium Stadium

2. MUSIC ACT

   The year they had their first number-one single was ...

   The cover of their first studio album depicts an ...

   In the video for the first hit, the singer walks ...

   Answer: Coldplay

3. SERIES OF NOVELS

It was written by ...

It is set in ...

The lead characters are called ...

Answer: *Twilight*

4. COUNTRY

The time here is usually ... hours ahead of Greenwich Mean Time

It borders ... other countries

It hosted the World Cup in ...

Answer: South Africa

5. NOVEL

It is set in ...

The plot involves a ...

One of the main characters is ...

Answer: *The Hound of the Baskervilles*

Useful answers would have been ...

1. 1999; Cardiff; retractable roof 2. Orange globe; 2008; along a beach 3. Stephenie Meyer; Forks, Washington; Edward and Bella 4. Two; six; 2010 5. London and Dartmoor; supposed family curse; a murderous dog

GAME 2

A BLAST FROM THE PAST TENSE

You need: nothing
Players: any number
Scoring: 2 points for each of your question; 1 point if you answer someone else's

AC: Now, this is one of those games where there's often more than one right answer. They have to put words into the past tense, but 'see' could be 'seen' or 'saw'. That's why I–

RO: Alan, is this going to be the conversation where you try and get the line 'And by "past tense" we're looking for the simple preterite, not anything in the form of a past participle' into the script? Again?

AC: I just think it would be a lot of fun for a teatime audience to hear a little about verb inflections ...

[pause]

AC: Fine, but then you'd better tell the readers how to adjudicate when someone gives an answer that's OK but not in the answer list.

RO: Over the years, you develop a kind of 'feel' for it, but it's hard to put into words.

AC: Really?

RO: No, not really. The advice is: remember it's only a game and don't be a jerk.

As happens so often, we're not looking for the actual answer here.

This time, after you've realised what the right answer is, you have to search it for any words that can be put into the past tense and ...

... put them in the past tense.

Take it in turns. Two points if you get your own question; if you don't, anyone else can pipe up and try and get 1 point.

1. **Which 2016 film was the third on-screen collaboration for Emma Stone and Ryan Gosling?**
2. **What widespread industrial action was called by the TUC on 3 May 1926?**
3. **What silly name does William James Adams use when rapping and judging talent shows?**
4. **Newcastle, Gateshead and Sunderland are in which metropolitan county, named after two rivers?**
5. **In 2019, Sara Cox took over from Jo Whiley and Simon Mayo in which slot on Radio 2?**
6. **What repetitive six-word phrase to introduce a joke was first recorded in the 1960s?**

7. **Which 2010 romantic comedy film starring Julia Roberts was adapted from a best-selling memoir subtitled *One Woman's Search for Everything across Italy, India and Indonesia*?**

8. **In the film *Moonraker*, Bond descends into the jungle using what form of transport?**

9. **Which stingy character, created by Roger Hargreaves, finds that his nose has been turned into a carrot as a punishment for his parsimoniousness?**

10. **Who was the woman mentioned in question one?**

Answers: (but accept variants as per the advice above: stricken, hanged, eaten, etc.) 1. La La Landed 2. General struck 3. would.i.was 4. Tyne and Wore 5. Drovetime 6. I said, I said, I said 7. Ate Prayed Loved 8. Hung glider 9. Mr Meant 10 Emma Stoned

GAME 3
SIZE MATTERS #3

You need: pencil and paper for each player
Players: any number
Scoring: see below

In this game, we give you a category and everyone writes down something they think is in that category.

You get 2 points if you've written the longest correct answer of all the guesses (count letters but not spaces, punctuation, etc.).

And you get 4 points if you've managed to find the longest of all the possible answers. We've listed them in order of bigness.

THE UNITED STATES OF AMERICA

(any of the 50)

Massachusetts
North Carolina
South Carolina
New Hampshire
Pennsylvania
West Virginia
Connecticut
Mississippi
North Dakota
Rhode Island
South Dakota
California
Washington
Louisiana
Minnesota
New Jersey
New Mexico

Tennessee
Wisconsin
Arkansas
Colorado
Delaware
Illinois
Kentucky
Maryland
Michigan
Missouri
Nebraska
Oklahoma
Virginia
Alabama
Arizona
Florida
Georgia

Indiana
Montana
New York
Vermont
Wyoming
Alaska
Hawaii
Kansas
Nevada
Oregon
Idaho
Maine
Texas
Iowa
Ohio
Utah

TOP 10 SINGLES BY WHITNEY HOUSTON

'I Wanna Dance with Somebody (Who Loves Me)'

'Could I Have This Kiss Forever'

'It's Not Right But It's Okay'

'Saving All My Love for You'

'The Greatest Love of All'

'I Will Always Love You'

'Love Will Save the Day'

'I'm Your Baby Tonight'

'Million Dollar Bill'

'My Love Is Your Love'

'One Moment in Time'

'If I Told You That'

'When You Believe'

'How Will I Know'

'I Have Nothing'

'I'm Every Woman'

'So Emotional'

ENDANGERED AND/OR VULNERABLE ANIMALS

(we're looking for any species listed by the WWF as Endangered or Vulnerable as we type)

Southern Rockhopper Penguin
North Atlantic Right Whale
Greater One-Horned Rhino
Borneo Pygmy Elephant
Ganges River Dolphin
Black Spider Monkey
Black-footed Ferret
Indus River Dolphin
Leatherback Turtle
Olive Ridley Turtle
Sri Lankan Elephant
Galápagos Penguin
Indochinese Tiger
Irrawaddy Dolphin
Loggerhead Turtle
African Elephant
Great White Shark
Mountain Gorilla
Savanna Elephant
African Wild Dog
Forest Elephant
Hector's Dolphin
Humphead Wrasse
Indian Elephant

Asian Elephant
Giant Tortoise
Hippopotamus
Marine Iguana
Bengal Tiger
Bluefin Tuna
Green Turtle
Snow Leopard
Bigeye Tuna
Chimpanzee
Giant Panda
Whale Shark
Amur Tiger
Blue Whale
Polar Bear
Sea Turtle
Fin Whale
Red Panda
Sea Lions
Sei Whale
Bonobo
Dugong
Tiger
Whale

NUMBERS BETWEEN 1 AND 50 INCLUSIVE

(as rendered in Roman numerals, and we're politely ignoring the tendency of some clockmakers to do their 4s as IIII)

	ΛXX	IΛXX
˥	XIX	IIΛX
X	IXX	IIIΛ
Λ	IIX	IIIΛX
I	ΛIX	III˥X
XI	IIΛ	IIΛXX
XX	III	IΛXXX
˥X	IXXX	ΛIXXX
ΛI	II˥X	IIΛ˥X
ΛX	IΛ˥X	XIXXX
IX	IIIX	IIXXX
II	ΛI˥X	IIΛXX
IΛ	XIXX	IIIXX
XXX	XI˥X	IIΛXXX
IΛX	ΛXXX	IIIΛ˥X
I˥X	ΛIXX	IIIXXX
Λ˥X	IIXX	IIIΛXXX

GAME 4

48-52

You need: nothing
Players: any number
Scoring: 2 points for every correct answer

AC: You know what I never really enjoy?

RO: Coming back from lunch on time? Clearing the stained coffee mugs from around your computer? Not doing crosswords in working hours?

AC: I was thinking of 'true-or-false' questions. Either you have to start a le Carré-style mind-game – 'What does the question setter think I'm *going* to answer, or is it a double-bluff?' – or it's basically down to luck: 50–50.

RO: Some people do like that kind of question, though ...

AC: Which is why we've come up with a twist here. The 48–52 game.

RO: Tell me there's nothing about the referend–

AC: Definitely not.

RO: Yeah, let's keep that out of the quiz. In fact, we should think about whether we ought to call it the 48–52 game.

AC: Actually, there might be one question that has a link to ... that thing.

For each of the questions below, decide which option is 52 per cent and which is 48 per cent.

1. Walking habits of UK adults

   More than a mile a day _____ _____ A mile a day or less

2. Items of veg eaten by British children

   Zero a day _____ _____ One or more a day

3. How people feel about the Grand National

   'It's very or fairly cruel' _____ _____ 'It's not cruel'

4. Young people's New Year resolutions

   Save money _____ _____ Something else

5. British people's response to a photograph of Trafalgar Square

   'That's Trafalgar Square' _____ _____ 'I don't know what that is'

6. Composition of Vietnam's roads

   Unpaved _____ _____ Paved

7. **Composition of Guam**

Forest _____ _____ Not forest

8. **Composition of seal milk, 20 days after pup is born**

Fat _____ _____ Everything that isn't fat

9. **Literacy level of Afghanistani men**

Literate _____ _____ Non-literate

10. **Vote of confidence in Theresa May, January 2019**

Confidence _____ _____ No confidence

Answers: 1. 48-52 2. 52-48 3. 52-48 4. 48-52 5. 48-52 6. 48-52
7. 48-52 8. 52-48 9. 52-48 10. 52-48

SET 13 SCORECARD				
	Player 1	Player 2	Player 3	Player 4
Game 1				
Game 2				
Game 3				
Game 4				
Totals				

WINNER!

SET 14

... in which you might start a grudge that lasts for years

GAME 1
WHERE IS KAZAKHSTAN? #1

You need: a phone or tablet each
Players: 2 or more
Scoring: 2 points for each correct answer

AC: Some of the viewers' favourite *House of Games* moments are where our contestants just don't know something they really should.

RO: Yeah. We tend to get those especially in the rounds where we've baked that into the format from the very first moment, Alan.

AC: We deliberately set out to cause mild embarrassment?

RO: Yes, but we probably shouldn't re-live any of those moments here.

AC: Agreed. Let's just say I was thinking of the time a ... distinguished public intellectual ...

RO: ... yep, tactfully done ...

AC: ... said where Tutankhamen's tomb was and was almost precisely 2,000 miles out.

RO: You have to wonder whether he or she now avoids eye-contact whenever an Egyptologist walks past his or her office.

AC: She probably hides and puts up a sign saying, 'Professor Williams is on a lecture tour.'

RO: So close.

Open a map app on your device, and pinch it until the named continent fills the screen.

Tap and hold where *you think* the named landmark is. Be careful, you only get one go at this.

Now ask for directions (on foot), and enter the name of the landmark as your destination. Compare your results: whoever is closest gets the 2 points each time. Remember to cancel everything before your next 'journey'.

1. **Continent: Asia**
   Destination: Taj Mahal

2. **Continent: Europe**
   Destination: Colosseum

3. **Continent: South America**
   Destination: Christ the Redeemer statue

4. **Continent: Africa**
   Destination: The Sphinx

5. **Continent: Europe**
   Destination: Nuneaton Town Hall

GAME 2

AND THE ANSWER ISN'T #4

You need: a smartphone or tablet; your House of Games Spoiler Blocker

Players: ideally 4; you could make it work with 2 but it's probably not worth it

Scoring: see below

These four questions are multiple-choice, but we haven't bothered to come up with the wrong ones. That's your job.

When it's your turn, everyone else looks at the question and its answer. Then (so that handwriting is no clue), someone takes the phone and types in (in random order) the right answer and a multi-choice option from each of the other players. (You shouldn't also type in any of the fun facts we offer as explanation.)

Then you get the phone, someone reads you the question, and you consider the options.

If you're right, you get a point. Obviously. But if you're wrong, the point goes to whoever invented the option you chose. Take your time...

1. **The English puritan politician Praise-God Barebones had a son called Nicholas. But what was Nicholas's middle name?**

   Answer: If-Christ-Had-Not-Died-For-Thee-Thou-Hadst-Been-Damned (Happy Christmas to all our readers, by the way)

2. **After a tank burst at a distilling company in Boston in 1919, 21 people were killed by a flood of what?**

   Answer: Molasses (more than 2 million gallons flooded the streets; it was over 100 years ago and so has passed from tragedy to quiz fodder, those are the rules)

3. **What is the name of the king penguin who lives at Edinburgh Zoo, who is also a Colonel-in-Chief of the Norwegian King's Guard?**

   Answer: Brigadier Sir Nils Olav

4. **After winning his Nobel Prize, Niels Bohr was given a house that had a built-in pipeline to supply him with free what?**

   Answer: Beer (there was a brewery next door)

GAME 3

THINK LIKE A QUESTION SETTER

You need: a smartphone or tablet for each player; your House of Games Spoiler Blocker

Players: 2 or more

Scoring: 5 points if you recover access to your device

AC: Do you know, I had to correct the Wikipedia section on Fictional Snails last week?* It didn't have Brian from *The Magic Roundabout*. Even though it *did* have a snail which appeared very briefly in *Angry Birds* and–

RO: Wait, you use Wikipedia?

AC: Um. We might use it to get an idea, but we always provide sources, even if that means contacting a very understanding market analyst at the Agriculture and Horticulture Development Board to find out whether the UK is a net importer or exporter of lamb.**

RO: Hm. Do you think our readers can imagine what it's like not just being able to look things up on their phones?

AC: Some of them are about to find out.

---

* This is true.

** This is also true; many thanks to Rebecca at AHDB

Unlock your device and go to the Password option in Settings. Disable recognition by face/thumbprint, etc. Get the device ready to receive a new numeric passcode.

Pass your device to the player on your left (swap if there are two of you, duh).

When it's your turn, use your House of Games Spoiler Blocker to reveal one of the Answer Sets below. Choose enough answers to create a new passcode, then enter it into the device you have been passed. Confirm the new passcode. (WRITE IT DOWN AS WELL in case you forget what you've chosen.)

Now pass the device back to its owner and give them the clues in the right order.

If they fail to regain access after two attempts, they must find out the answers using pre-phone technology. Welcome to how we used to live.

ANSWER SET ONE

Four cubed: 64
Shirt number worn by Lionel Messi, Pelé and Diego Maradona: 10
Date in July of Bastille Day: 14

ANSWER SET TWO

Square root of 289: 17
Number of players on a basketball court: 10
Number of months in WW2 (not including the one extra day): 72

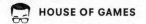

ANSWER SET THREE

Square root of 324: 18
Number furthest left on a dartboard: 11
Number of prime ministers from Heath to May including both: 10

ANSWER SET FOUR

Three cubed: 27
Matches played, World Cup 2018: 64
Queen + her children + her grandchildren = ?: 13

ANSWER SET FIVE

Square root of 196: 14
Number of players, rugby league team: 13
Number of calendar years *during which* Thatcher was prime minister: 12

ANSWER SET SIX

Square root of 361: 19
Number of kilometres in marathon (rounded): 42
Number of kings named George or Edward who have ruled England (since the Norman Conquest): 14

GAME 4
BUILD YOUR OWN QUESTION #1

You need: nothing
Players: 1 question-reader, 2 players or teams
Scoring: 1 point for every correct answer

AC: We don't seem to play Build Your Own Question so often nowadays.

RO: Yeah, I–

AC: It's a shame, that. It's so satisfying when you complete a set of 16 questions that fit all 8 categories. For the team, it's a genuine masterclass in question-setting.

RO: Yeah, but nobody cares.

AC: ?

RO: Hm, I may have put that a little bluntly. I mean, I think most people just try to answer a question and don't necessarily think, 'Golly gee, this has been written under some self-imposed constraints which have somehow not resulted in editorial compromise.' Plus it's annoying that most of the questions don't get used.

AC: We could re-format it for the book, though! In a way that does use all the questions?

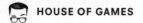

RO: You love those questions, don't you?

AC: I really, really do.

The question-asker reads out the four categories along the columns and the four down the rows. (If the question-asker is you, you should probably encourage them to write down the categories, and tick off what's been answered, unless you especially enjoy people asking 'What are the categories again?' and 'Have we already had Molluscs and Peter Kay?')

Taking it in turns, each player/team chooses one category from *each* group of four and the question-asker gives them the question that's in *both* categories. Repeat until all 16 questions have been asked and answered.

	1980s POP	PRIME MINISTERS	CHILDREN'S BOOKS	SCOTLAND
FRIENDS	Which group had a 1988 UK number-one hit in aid of Childline with a cover of 'With a Little Help from My Friends'?	'I wish everyone, friend or foe, well. That is that, the end.' Whose final words to Parliament as prime minister were these?	In *Thomas & Friends: Engines to the Rescue!*, which of Thomas's friends is the 'Red Engine'?	The 2018 film *Mary, Queen of Scots* imagines a friendship between Mary and whom?
FORGETFULNESS	The song 'Don't You (Forget About Me)' featured in which 1985 Brat Pack film?	In 2015, David Cameron said he'd rather that people 'supported West Ham', after apparently forgetting that he supports which team?	What is the name of the 'Forgetful Cat', created by Judith Kerr, who has featured in 17 books since 1970?	The famous poem that begins 'Should auld acquaintance be forgot' is traditionally credited to which writer?
COUGHS & SNEEZES	In which Police hit single does Sting rhyme 'cough' with 'Nabokov'?	Theresa May's 2017 party conference speech was marred by a cough, letters falling off her backdrop and a comedian giving her what?	In the book by Roger Hargreaves, Mr Sneeze's nose is red. What colour is the rest of him?	Complete this line from an old rhyme heard in Scotland: 'Sneeze on a Monday, sneeze for danger; sneeze on a Tuesday ...'
IMAGINARY CREATURES	Ten years after its original release, 'Heaven Must Be Missing an Angel' was a 1986 hit for which disco outfit?	In 2018 there were petitions for images of Harry Maguire riding a unicorn and Margaret Thatcher to appear where?	The Gruffalo has knobbly knees as well as turned-out toes. Where is its poisonous wart?	In Scottish folklore, a selkie can shift between human form and that of which mammal?

Answers

	1980s POP	PRIME MINISTERS	CHILDREN'S BOOKS	SCOTLAND
FRIENDS	Wet Wet Wet	Tony Blair	James	Elizabeth I
FORGETFUL-NESS	*The Breakfast Club*	Aston Villa	Mog	Robert Burns
COUGHS & SNEEZES	'Don't Stand So Close To Me'	A P45	Blue	'…kiss a stranger'
IMAGINARY CREATURES	Tavares	The £50 note	At the end of its nose	Seal

SET 14 SCORECARD				
	Player 1	Player 2	Player 3	Player 4
Game 1				
Game 2				
Game 3				
Game 4				
Totals				

WINNER!

SET 15

... in which you will discover you've been saying an animal's name wrong

GAME 1

SEE MY GUESTS #3&4

You need: your House of Games Spoiler Blocker
Players: any number
Scoring: see below

AC: That game It's All In The Name can be a tricky one to write for. Finding answers from the letters in a contestant's name, I mean.

RO: Some names are better than others, right?

AC: Yep. Sometimes you can find a word, but it doesn't make for a question with any character. Say we had on that rapper, G-Unit. Not much to work with. What are you going to do for GNU? 'Another name for the wildebeest'? Snore.

RO: There's that old song: I'm a ger-noo...

AC: I see what you're saying! OK, so *here*'s a great question ...

Animal whose name is often
mis-pronounced with a 'G' at
the beginning because that's
how it was sung in 1957 song
by Flanders and Swann

... wait, how many lines of text does the screen hold again?

RO: I'm pretty sure G-Unit are a band, not a person.

In this game, you work together.

You'll see two images of guests from the TV version of *House of Games*. If you can tell who they are straightaway, that's *10 points each*. (Get someone else to check, in case you're wrong.)

If you can't, then there are some nice straightforward questions underneath that we wrote for the It's All In The Name round. As that name suggests, this will give you some of the letters of the guest's name. But each time you use one of these questions, *the points available go down by 2*.

Cooperation and inspiration: and you'll all boost your scores.

GUEST THREE

For 10 points:

Can you name him?

Answer these questions to get some of the letters in his name.

For 8 points:

1980s sitcom set in Maplin's holiday camp

Answer: Hi-De-Hi!

For 6 points:

Country which moved its capital from Lagos to Abuja in 1991

Answer: Nigeria

For 4 points:

Salad dressing typically made using buttermilk, mayonnaise, garlic, onion and seasonings

Answer: Ranch

For 2 points:

Major river that flows through Vaduz, Basel and Düsseldorf

Answer: Rhine

Answer: Richard Herring

GUEST FOUR

For 10 points:

Can you name her?

Answer these questions to get some of the letters in her name.

For 8 points:

Ruth Jones sitcom set in fictional South Wales Valleys village of Pontyberry

Answer: *Stella*

For 6 points:

Musical with songs 'Stranger in Paradise' and 'Baubles, Bangles and Beads'

Answer: *Kismet*

For 4 points:

Name of Nyasaland, post-independence

Answer: Malawi

For 2 points:

Substance with a pH level above seven

Answer: Alkali

Answer: Kate Williams

GAME 2
ALL IN THE DETAILS #2

You need: possibly pencil and paper; your House of Games Spoiler Blocker
Players: 2 or more
Scoring: see below

Take it in turns to reveal one of the Detail Sets below. If you want to keep this book pristine, write out the details on a piece of paper. Fill in the gaps with a few words. If you don't know the precise information – well, that's part of the fun. Put your best guess. (But don't put any of the words of the answer.)

Now, read out your completed Detail Set to the other players. Once you get to the end, everyone has as many guesses as they like. (Take it in turns or shout out depending how rambunctious you're feeling.)

If a player gets it right, they get a point – and so do you.

(By the way, we've also given what might have been the most useful answers – see below, but if you peek, you're missing the point of this game and, to be honest, games in general.)

1. WORK OF ART

It can be seen in ...

It was started in the year ...

It depicts ... figures

Answer: The Last Supper

2. HISTORICAL EVENT

It took place in the year ...

It was fought to contest the ... throne

It was lost by ...

Answer: Battle of Culloden

3. SPORTING EVENT

It takes place in the month of ...

The decade it first took place was the ...

The winners receive the ...

Answer: The Super Bowl

4. LANDMARK

It is in the country of ...

In 1987 it was made a ...

It was first 'conquered' in ...

Answer: Kilimanjaro

5. TV PROGRAMME

Its usual timeslot is …

Its prizes have included …

It is best described as …

Answer: *Richard Osman's House of Games*

Useful answers would have been …

1. An Italian convent; 1495; 13 2. 1746; British; the Jacobites 3. February; 1960s; Vince Lombardi Trophy 4. Tanzania; UNESCO World Heritage site; 1889 5. 6pm; Wikipedia, as ever, has a comprehensive list, unless some killjoy has deemed the information non-encyclopædic; we're sure whatever you said is brilliant

GAME 3

BUILD YOUR OWN QUESTION #2

You need: nothing
Players: 1 question-reader, 2 players or teams
Scoring: 1 point for every correct answer

The question-asker reads out the four categories along the columns and the four down the rows. (If the question-asker is you, you should probably encourage them to write them down, and tick off what's been answered, unless you enjoy people asking 'What are the categories again?' and 'Have we already had Candy Crush and The Crimean War?')

Taking it in turns, each player/team chooses one category from each group of four and the question-asker gives them the question that's in both categories. Repeat until all 16 questions have been asked and answered.

	MUSIC OF THE 1970s	SPAIN	CHILDREN'S TOYS & GAMES	HORSES & PONIES
THREE-LETTER PALINDROMES	'Abba' is a palindrome, as is the three-letter title of which of their UK top-ten hits?	Which of these is the Spanish word for gold: *ojo, oro, oso or ovo*?	What three-letter palindrome means a dot on a domino?	What three-letter palindrome is a word for a light, two-wheeled horse-drawn carriage?
THE WEATHER	What weather word appears in the titles of top-ten hits for Elkie Brooks and Stevie Wonder?	According to a song in *My Fair Lady*, where is the majority of the precipitation on the east of the Iberian peninsula?	What form of children's toy is used as a meteorological instrument by the British Antarctic Survey?	In the song 'A Horse With No Name', what weather is the narrator glad to have escaped?
MERRY CHRISTMAS!	Which UK comedy trio had a 1975 hit with 'Make a Daft Noise for Christmas'?	In a traditional Catalan nativity scene, the figure known as a 'Caganer' is traditionally depicted doing what?	Who wrote about the toys he had received at Christmas in his memoir *A Child's Christmas in Wales*?	The full version of which Christmassy song describes a couple meeting by accident while being pulled in the snow by a horse?
WHODUNNITS	Which 1978 song features a brawl in a nightclub and a mystery over who fired gunshots?	Seeking privacy in 1927, Agatha Christie travelled to Puerto de la Cruz on which Spanish island?	Which Cluedo character was 'killed off' in 2016 and replaced with the scientist Dr Orchid?	Whose first novel, *Dead Cert*, opens with a death at a Maidenhead steeplechase?

Answers:

	MUSIC OF THE 1970s	SPAIN	CHILDREN'S TOYS & GAMES	HORSES & PONIES
THREE-LETTER PALINDROMES	SOS	*Oro*	Pip	Gig
THE WEATHER	Sunshine	The plain	Kite	The rain
MERRY CHRISTMAS!	The Goodies	Having a poo	Dylan Thomas	'Jingle Bells'
WHODUNNITS	'Copacabana'	Tenerife	Mrs White	Dick Francis

GAME 4

THE NICE ROUND - PEOPLE

You need: pencil and paper; your House of Games Spoiler Blocker
Players: ideally 4
Scoring: see below

Position your House of Games Spoiler Blocker so that only the first name is visible.

Now, take it in turns to be the Guesser. Each time, everyone who isn't the Guesser reads the answer and writes down a one-word clue to help the Guesser.

After the Guesser has been shown all three clues, they give their guess. They get a point if they're right, and also award a point to whichever player they think has been most helpful.

The Guesser should remember that the other players might make mistakes, like when Michael Buerk quite reasonably guessed 'Dick Turpin' based on Elis James's clue 'Highwayman'. (The answer was 'Dick Whittington' and Elis did not get awarded a point for being the most helpful.)

THE PEOPLE

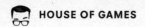

Jessica Ennis-Hill

Plato

Mikhail Gorbachev

Linda McCartney

Condoleezza Rice

Ludwig van Beethoven

Kublai Khan

Marilyn Monroe

SET 15 SCORECARD				
	Player 1	Player 2	Player 3	Player 4
Game 1				
Game 2				
Game 3				
Game 4				
Totals				

WINNER! ______________________________

SET 16

... in which you will be impressed by the Pope

GAME 1
THE REAL MCCOY

You need: your House of Games Spoiler Blocker
Players: any number
Scoring: 4 points for the first to spot each Real McCoy

Four pictures. But which is the Real McCoy?

A COD

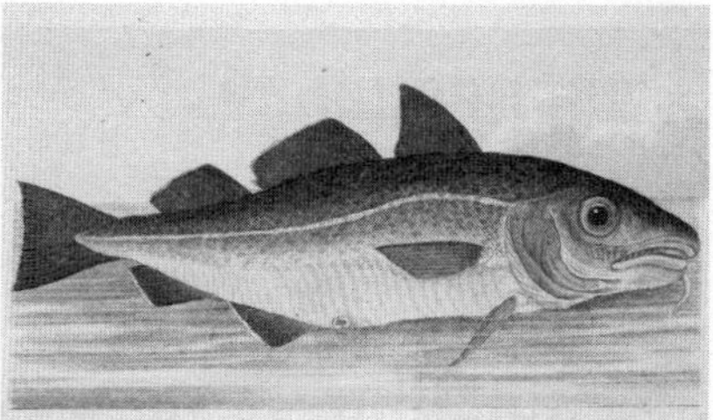

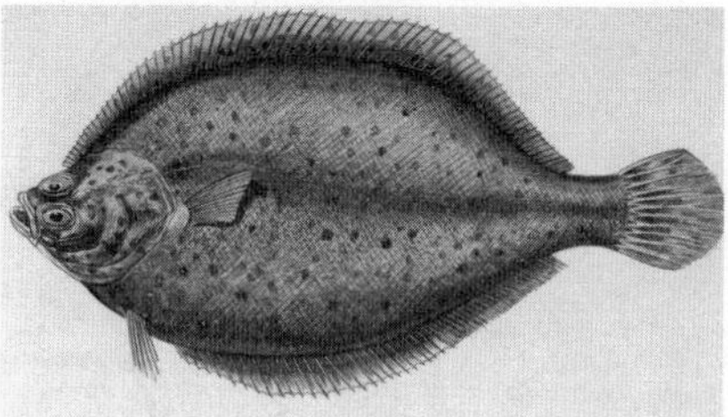

Answer: C

STREET SIGN IN *EASTENDERS*

LONDON BOROUGH OF WARFORD
ALBERT SQUARE
E20

LONDON BOROUGH OF WALFORD
ALBERT SQUARE
SE20

LONDON BOROUGH OF WALFORD
ALBERT SQUARE
E20

LONDON BOROUGH OF WALFORD
ALBERT SQUARE
E17

Answer: C

THE OUTLINE OF THE FALKLAND ISLANDS

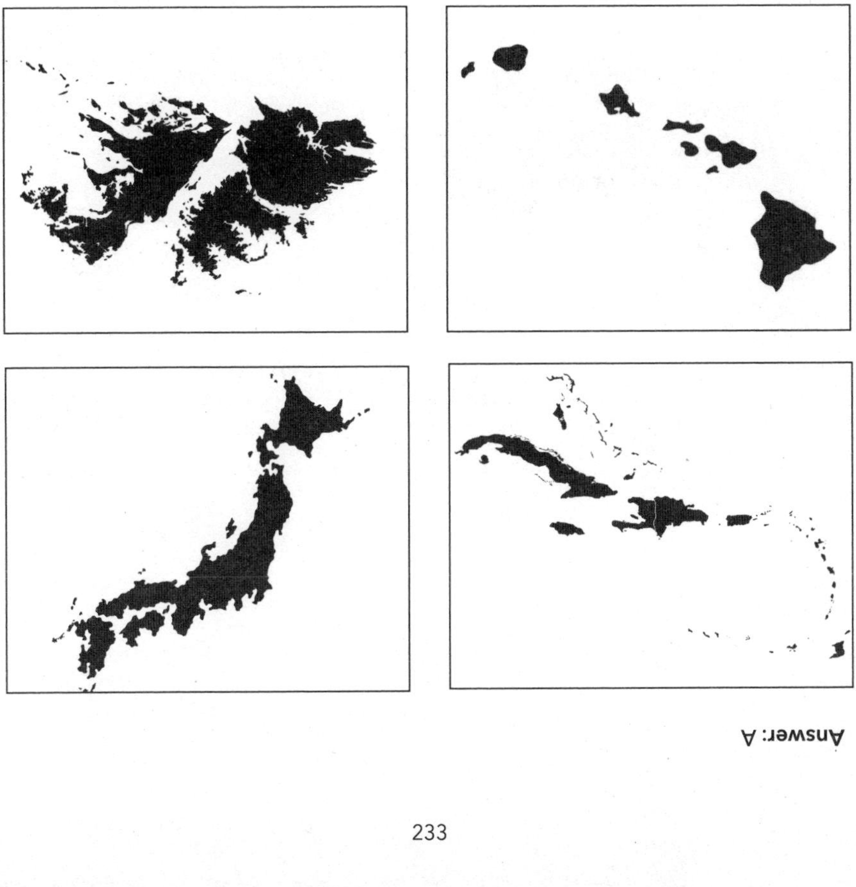

Answer: A

PERSON SUCCEEDED BY JUSTIN TRUDEAU

Answer: A

CORRECTLY WIRED PLUG

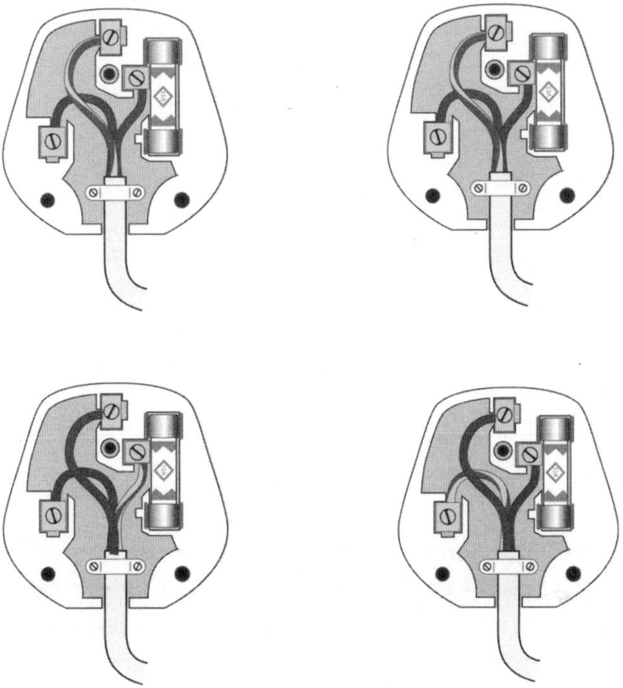

Answer: B

GAME 2

AND THE ANSWER ISN'T #5

You need: a smartphone or tablet; your House of Games Spoiler Blocker

Players: ideally 4; you could make it work with 2 but it's probably not worth it

Scoring: see below

These four questions are multiple-choice, but we haven't bothered to come up with the wrong ones. That's your job.

When it's your turn, everyone else looks at the question and its answer. Then (so that handwriting is no clue), someone takes the phone and types in (in random order) the right answer and a multi-choice option from each of the other players. (You shouldn't also type in any of the fun facts we offer as explanation.)

Then you get the phone, someone reads you the question, and you consider the options.

If you're right, you get a point. Obviously. But if you're wrong, the point goes to whoever invented the option you chose. Take your time ...

1. **What did Robert Louis Stevenson bequeath to a fifteen-year-old named Anne Ide when he had no use for it himself?**

   Answer: His birthday (Anne's own birthday was on Christmas Day, which she didn't enjoy, so Stevenson passed on to her his birthday of 13 November)

2. **Before his Vatican stint, Pope Francis's former employers include a nightclub. What was his job?**

   Answer: Bouncer

3. **How did Virginia Woolf describe James Joyce's novel *Ulysses*?**

   Answer: 'A queasy undergraduate scratching his pimples'

4. **At Ramsbottom's annual World Black Pudding Throwing Championship, players hurl their black puddings at what?**

   Answer: Yorkshire puddings (in jocose reference to the Wars of the Roses)

GAME 3
DOUBLE-SCREENING IT

You need: your House of Games Spoiler Blocker
Players: any number
Scoring: see below

AC: This game is fun to play but would create all kinds of legal issues if we did it on the TV. We're happy, though, to pass those issues on to you at home. So remember, before you start, to find out the composer and publisher for each of the tunes below, get their contact details, and obtain permission to adapt their works. Make sure the agreement covers international territories, in case you want to play the game abroad, and when it comes to moral rights–

RO: Alan, you know they don't have to do any of that, right?

AC: Yeah. I just thought a bit of recognition for the hard work of the backstage team was in order. I've made my little point. OK, have fun everyone!

This game is best played in pairs, but feel free to just take it turns performing to the group.

We're going to give you names of TV shows, in pairs. When it's your turn, you have to sing the words of the first show to the theme tune of the second show. If your partner gets *both* titles correct, you each get 2 points. No half marks here.

Our tip is to wordlessly hum the theme tune in your head before you start. But if you want to just jump in and make an idiot of yourself, it's a free country.

1. Tune: the classic *ITV News at Ten*

   'It's in a *wood* / It's got the Wot-tin-gers / A lovely *wood* / It's got the Pon-tip-ines / Eve-ry. One. Go. To. Sleep'

   Answer: *In The Night Garden*

2. Tune: *Batman*

   'Julie Jenny Janet Jackie / Carole Chizzy Cilla Coleen / TALKING / Lynda Lisa Lorna Lesley / Stacey Sheree Sally Shirley / TALKING'

   Answer: *Loose Women*

3. Tune: *The Simpsons*

   'Week after week, we're in a diff-er-ent town / Some-where like Tun-bridge WELLS' (ignore the whirly bit) 'Five diff-er-ent folk talk-ing each other down' (again ignore the whirly bit)

   Answer: *Question Time*

4. Tune: *Doctor Who*

   (for the dun-dah-dahs) 'Co-sy chat, co-sy chat, co-sy chat / Co-sy chat, co-sy chat, co-sy chat'
   (for the high bit) 'And now / We'll see / How con-men prey on'
   (back to the dun-dah-dahs) 'Pen-sion-ers, pen-sion-ers, pen-sion-ers'

   Answer: *The One Show*

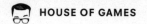

5. Tune: *Friends*

   I never knew my great-grandpa had seven wives / I wish I'd never visited the National Archives / Why couldn't granddad show more loyalty? / I really thought that I'd find out my ancestors were royalty

   Answer: *Who Do You Think You Are?*

6. Tune: *Strictly Come Dancing*

   'It was not so long ago, but it seems so weird / Medicine was different then, it was often feared / E-*pi*-dur-*als* weren't nearly quite so *com*-mon then and / Though they've got the NHS, it's / Only just appeared'

   Answer: *Call the Midwife*

GAME 4

THE ANSWER'S IN THE QUESTION #1

You need: nothing
Players: any number
Scoring: 2 for each correct answer (if scoring)

In this game, we've been generous enough to give you a clue *and* the answer.

In case you don't find the simple act of reading each answer aloud satisfying, we've jumbled them up. The words in **bold type** can be jumbled up to give each answer, which is also described by the clue as a whole.

You'll probably want to gather round the book and do this together. But if you insist, someone can read them out and you can get competitive.

ITEMS OF CLOTHING

1. Your **anklets**, but not your bracelets, are shielded from view by this roomy garment.

2. In these loosely cut trousers, a **strap can go** across the large pockets.

3. There is a **surplus of** this variety of knickerbockers at golf courses.

4. You should ensure that the wool of this garment **isn't wet** before you put on either of its two pieces.

5. If your upper body begins to **glisten** in the heat, you might strip down to this garment.

UK MAGAZINES

1. Celebrities used to **hate** appearing in this magazine's Circle Of Shame feature.

2. Diets, competitions and celebs can **all be** found in this weekly magazine.

3. This magazine's **editors aim** to help you make good choices on a night in.

4. Pretty much anything might appear in this magazine: **karate, bake sales** - you name it.

5. Of a Wetherspoon and the Waldorf, this magazine is more likely to be spotted in the **latter**.

Answers:

Items of Clothing

1. Slanket 2. Cargo pants 3. Plus-fours 4. Twinset 5. Singlet

UK Magazines

1. *Heat* 2. *Bella* 3. *Radio Times* 4. *Take a Break* 5. *Tatler*

SET 16 SCORECARD				
	Player 1	Player 2	Player 3	Player 4
Game 1				
Game 2				
Game 3				
Game 4				
Totals				

WINNER! ____

SET 17

... in which you will tsk-tsk at Winston Churchill

GAME 1
FIVES ALIVES - SPORT

You need: nothing
Players: any number
Scoring: no points - work together

RO: Here's another 'Fives Alives', but this one is about sport, so I know a lot of you will very happily ignore it. But it's a good one. If you like sport. I take your point though, if you don't like sport, it's really bad.

Here again are some top fives, and the initial letters of the answers - but can you fill in those gaps?

(The time of typing is March 2019, so ignore any records that have been broken or medals returned between April and Christmas)

A) THE LOWEST RANKED EUROPEAN MEN'S FOOTBALL NATIONS

1. **SM**
2. **G**
3. **M**
4. **L**
5. **M**

B) SURNAMES OF UK SPORTSPEOPLE WITH THE MOST OLYMPIC MEDALS (SINCE 1945)

1. W (8)
2. H (7)
3. K (7)
4. R (6)
5. A (5)

C) SURNAMES OF THE FIVE WOMEN WITH THE MOST TENNIS GRAND-SLAM TITLES

1. W (23)
2. G (22)
3. N (18)
4. E (18)
5. C (11)

D) SURNAMES OF THE FIVE MEN WHO HAVE MADE THE MOST PRIZE MONEY IN THE HISTORY OF GOLF

1. W
2. M
3. S
4. F
5. J

E) SURNAMES OF BOWLERS WITH THE MOST CRICKET TEST WICKETS

1. M (800)
2. W (708)
3. K (619)
4. A (575)
5. M (563)

Answers:

A) San Marino, Gibraltar, Malta, Liechtenstein, Moldova
B) Wiggins, Hoy, (Jason) Kenny, Redgrave, Ainslie
C) (Serena) Williams, Graf, Navratilova, Evert, Court
D) Woods, Mickelson, Singh, Furyk, (Dustin) Johnson
E) Muralitharan, Warne, Kumble, Anderson, McGrath

GAME 2

WHAT'S THE GOLDEN RULE?

You need: nothing
Players: any number
Scoring: 2 points for every correct answer, bonus of 4 points for spotting the golden rule

When it's your turn, get someone to ask you questions from one of the packs below. Following a wrong guess, younger players are given the correct answer; grown-ups are not.

After answering three questions, you try to get a bonus by spotting the golden rule that connects the answers. For example, if the answers were BLITZ, QUARTZ and WALTZ, the golden rule would be that they all end in Z.

These are not quite as obvious as that – and in fact they get tougher as they go along.

QUESTION PACK 1

1. **Which element has the chemical symbol Ag?**

   Answer: Silver

2. **Which organs of a duck or goose are used to make *pâté de foie gras*?**

   Answer: Livers

3. **And while we're speaking French, what's the French for 'books' (not exercise books, which, as we all know, are *cahiers*)?**

   Answer: Livres

4. **What's the golden rule?**

   Answer: They are all anagrams of each other

QUESTION PACK 2

1. **Which of the gifts brought by the Three Wise Men was a fragrant gum resin taken from a tree?**

   Answer: Myrrh

2. **What underground room of a church gives its name to a tricky kind of crossword?**

   Answer: Crypt

3. **What kind of large cat gives its name to a range of strong-smelling deodorants?**

   Answer: Lynx

4. **What's the golden rule?**

   Answer: None of these contains any of the vowels A, E, I, O or U

QUESTION PACK 3

1. **What type of extinct mammoth is known as *Mammuthus primigenius*?**

   Answer: Woolly

2. **In what form does a scorpion appear on David Dimbleby's shoulder?**

   Answer: Tattoo

3. **In an orchestra, which other double-reed woodwinds usually sit behind the oboes?**

   Answer: Bassoons

4. **What's the golden rule?**

   Answer: They all have two double letters next to each other (if the player says, 'They all have OO in them', congratulate them for spotting it - but ask for more)

QUESTION PACK 4

1. **What French word for 'jewel' is used by estate agents to describe a small home?**

   Answer: *Bijou*

2. **Also known as a diacritic, what part of a letter might be acute, grave or circumflex?**

   Answer: Accent

3. **The name of what flowery fabric comes from a Sanskrit word for gaily coloured?**

   Answer: Chintz

4. **What's the golden rule?**

   Answer: The letters of the answer are in alphabetical order

GAME 3
BROKEN KARAOKE #2

You need: nothing
Players: 2 or more (plus one to read out the questions)
Scoring: 2 points for every correct answer

If you're reading the questions, first give the year. Then read out the initials to the lyrics from a well-known passage in a well-known pop song. Try to match them to how the song sounds (e.g. if the song contains a very long 'yeeeeeeeeeaaaaaaaaaaaaah', say a simple 'Y', then wait until giving the next letter).

TRY TO STAY ON ONE NOTE. This is not a game about melody. It's pure words, all the way.

If you don't know a song, skip it (or give it your best shot).

And if they don't get it the first time, just read it again ...

1. Year: 1979

   B E
   B L F
   B E
   H C Y C A F
   H C T L T B S B
   S B S P
   B E

2. Year: sometime in the early 1900s, probably

OWTS
GMI
WTSGMI
OLIWTBITN
WTSGMI

3. Year: 1987

O
IWDWS
IWFTHWS
Y
IWDWS
WSWLM

4. Year: 1971

ANSWSG
ATHJANH
ATSGA
AIKIKIKIKIKIKIKIKIKIKIKIKIKIKIKIKIKIKI
KIKIKIKIKIKIKIK

5. Year: 1745

GSOGQ
LLONQ
GSTQ

Answers: 1. 'Bright Eyes' 2. 'When the Saints Go Marching in' 3. 'I Wanna Dance with Somebody (Who Loves Me)' 4. 'Ain't No Sunshine' 5. 'God Save the Queen'

GAME 4
DISTINCTLY AVERAGE #2

You need: pencil and paper; a phone, or someone who's good with numbers

Players: 4, 6, 8, 10 ... basically, an even number that's 4 or more

Scoring: 2 points for every win

Sort yourselves into pairs.

For the rules, see Game 2, Page 18: A Distinctly Average Christmas.

A Distinctly Average Christmas. This is one, though, that you can play at any time of year.

1. **In today's money, how much did Winston Churchill's household spend on wine each year between 1908 and 1914, as reported in the history book *No More Champagne: Churchill and His Money* by David Lough?**

2. **According to the NASA Voyager website, how far away, in kilometres, is *Voyager 1*, the farthest artificial object from Earth?**

3. **According to the UK Cinema Association, how many cinemas were there in the UK in 2017?**

4. **How many athletes were selected to represent Team GB at the Rio 2016 Olympic Games?**

5. **In all of Shakespeare's plays combined, how many human on-stage deaths are there?**

Answers:

1. £90,679.75 (yes, and he also spent a lot on Havana cigars and polo ponies)
2. 20,750,540,609 (launched in 1977, it takes over 38 hours for a message to get there and back)
3. Just 801
4. 366
5. A macabre 74

SET 17 SCORECARD				
	Player 1	Player 2	Player 3	Player 4
Game 1				
Game 2				
Game 3				
Game 4				
Totals				

WINNER!

SET 18

... in which you will type a 58-letter word into your phone

GAME 1

SEE MY GUESTS #5&6

You need: your House of Games Spoiler Blocker
Players: any number
Scoring: see below

AC: You know I was talking about It's All In The Name?

RO: I was with you until something about wildebeests.

AC: Well, the trickiest names are the shortest ones. Like Amol Rajan. I mean, the longest answer you're going to get is, let's see ...

RO: Hm ... Actually, there must be a better example.

In this game, you work together.

You'll see two images of guests from the TV version of *House of Games*. If you can tell who they are straightaway, that's *10 points each*. (Get someone else to check, in case you're wrong.)

If you can't, then there are some nice straightforward questions underneath that we wrote for the It's All In The Name round. As that name suggests, this will give you some of the letters of the guest's name. But each time you use one of these questions, *the points available go down by 2*.

Cooperation and inspiration: and you'll all boost your scores.

GUEST FIVE

For 10 points:

Can you name her?

Answer these questions to get some of the letters in her name.

For 8 points:

Director of the Wallis Simpson bio-pic *W.E.*

Answer: Madonna

For 6 points:

Bronze Age civilisation from the island of Crete

Answer: Minoan

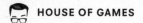

For 4 points:

Boy suspected of being the Antichrist in 1976 film *The Omen*

Answer: Damien

For 2 points:

Gland-like nasal tissue that's part of a child's immune system

Answer: Adenoid

Answer: Anne Diamond

GUEST SIX

For 10 points:

Can you name him?

Answer these questions to get some of the letters in his name.

For 8 points:

Type of building where 'something nasty' was apparently seen in the novel *Cold Comfort Farm*

Answer: Woodshed

For 6 points:

Columbo's long-time department in *Columbo*

Answer: Homicide

For 4 points:

Surname of film comedian with catchphrase 'Mr Grimsdale!'

Answer: Wisdom

For 2 points:

Order of knights including Obi-Wan Kenobi and Yoda

Answer: Jedi(s)

Answer: Josh Widdicombe

GAME 2

UNLUCKY FOR SOME #2

You need: 4 things numbered 1-4; a bag

Players: 4 (take in turns to ask questions or have a fifth player do that)

Scoring: 2 points for every correct answer

In this game, you might be lucky, and you might not.

First, read out a question.

Then, each player draws a number from a bag (see above). Whoever draws '1' gets to guess first. Whoever draws '2' gets to guess second. You *must* be able to guess what happens to the other players.

Going first means you've definitely got a chance of getting those 2 points, but going later means a wrong option or two have already been eliminated ...

1. Which of these people has achieved the EGOT, meaning they have won Emmy, Grammy, Oscar and Tony awards?

   John Legend

   Julie Andrews

   Elton John

   Lin-Manuel Miranda

2. Which of these technology entrepreneurs did *not* drop out of university?

   Jeff Bezos

   Mark Zuckerberg

   Steve Jobs

   Michael Dell

3. Which of these football clubs did David Beckham end his playing career at?

   AC Milan

   Paris Saint-Germain

   LA Galaxy

   Inter Milan

4. Which of these film roles *didn't* win Daniel Day-Lewis a Best Actor Oscar?

   Lincoln (2012)

   My Left Foot (1989)

   There Will Be Blood (2007)

   Gangs of New York (2002)

5. **Upon winning the Munich Open in 2015, Andy Murray was given what?**

    Stein of pilsner

    Cow

    Pair of lederhosen

    Honorary German citizenship

Answers: 1. John Legend (though hopefully by the time you play this, Julie will have her Tony, Lin-Manuel his Oscar and Elt his Emmy) 2. Jeff Bezos stuck it out at Princeton 3. Paris Saint-Germain 4. *Gangs of New York* (lost to Adrien Brody in *The Pianist*) 5. Lederhosen (which he put on immediately) and a fancy German car (which was not brought on to the court)

GAME 3

WHERE IS KAZAKHSTAN? #2

You need: a phone or tablet each
Players: 2 or more
Scoring: 2 points for each correct answer

Open a map app on your device, and pinch it until the named continent fills the screen.

Tap and hold where *you think* the named landmark is. Be careful, you only get one go at this.

Now ask for directions (on foot), and enter the name of the landmark as your destination. Compare your results: whoever is closest gets the 2 points each time. Remember to cancel everything before your next 'journey'.

1. Continent: Asia
   Destination: Mount Fuji

2. Continent: Africa
   Destination: Mount Kilimanjaro

3. Continent: Australasia
   Destination: Uluru/Ayers Rock

4. **Continent: North America**
   Destination: The Alamo

5. **Continent: Europe**
   Destination: Llanfairpwllgwyngyllgogerychwyrndrobwllllantysiliogogogoch

GAME 4

AND THE ANSWER ISN'T #6

You need: a smartphone or tablet; your House of Games Spoiler Blocker

Players: ideally 4; you could make it work with 2 but it's probably not worth it

Scoring: see below

These four questions are multiple-choice, but we haven't bothered to come up with the wrong ones. That's your job.

When it's your turn, everyone else looks at the question and its answer. Then (so that handwriting is no clue), someone takes the phone and types in (in random order) the right answer and a multi-choice option from each of the other players. (You shouldn't also type in any of the fun facts we offer as explanation.)

Then you take the phone, someone reads you the question, and you consider the options.

If you're right, you get a point. Obviously. But if you're wrong, the point goes to whoever invented the option you chose. Take your time …

1. **What is the official motto of the Thames Valley Police?**

   Answer: Let There Be Peace in the Thames Valley

2. **In July 2003, what was presented to Roger Federer from the organisers of the Swiss Open for winning his first Wimbledon title?**

   Answer: A cow (he called her Juliette)

3. **In 2017, owing to the colour of its large claw, a newly discovered species of shrimp was named after which band?**

   Answer: Pink Floyd

4. **What was Queen Victoria's first name?**

   Answer: Alexandrina

SET 18 SCORECARD				
	Player 1	Player 2	Player 3	Player 4
Game 1				
Game 2				
Game 3				
Game 4				
Totals				

WINNER! ______________________________

SET 19

... in which Richard expresses a controversial opinion about confectionery

GAME 1

THE NICE ROUND – PLACES

You need: pencil and paper; your House of Games Spoiler Blocker

Players: ideally 4

Scoring: see below

Position your House of Games Spoiler Blocker so that only the first place is visible.

Now, take it in turns to be the Guesser. Each time, everyone who isn't the Guesser reads the answer and writes down a one-word clue to help the Guesser.

After the Guesser has been shown all three clues, they give their guess. They get a point if they're right, and also award a point to whichever player they think has been most helpful.

THE PLACES

Bath

Mississippi

Rome

York

The Natural History Museum

The Andes

Sandringham

Saturn

GAME 2

CHRISTMAS RHYME TIME

You need: noise-makers
Players: any number plus someone to read the paired clues
Scoring: 2 points for every win

RO: Rhyme Time is one of my favourite rounds on *House Of Games*. Duke Ellington; Beef Wellington. Angela Merkel; the Arctic Circle. It's just very satisfying.

However, I've never really had the opportunity to write a round. Until now.

Here is my Christmas-themed Rhyme Time. I am annoyed that, for obvious reasons, I wasn't allowed to use my favourite Christmas item in this rhyming round. The Terry's Chocolate Orange.

Reader-outer: you will read a pair of clues. Players should buzz in when they can give both answers (which rhyme). They must give both!

1.

a) **Seasonally explosive cardboard tube**

b) **Chain of Mexican restaurants which most people seem to like, but which I've never really enjoyed**

Answer: Christmas cracker/Wahaca

2.

a) Gift from the Three Wise Men which is the hardest to spell

b) Britpop band

Answer: Myrrh/Blur

3.

a) Band with Christmas number one in 1973

b) Wimbledon singles champion in 1977

Answer: Slade/Virginia Wade

4.

a) Christmas bird

b) Largest city of New Mexico

Answer: Turkey/Albuquerque

5.

a) Rapper famous for 'Lose Yourself' and 'Stan'

b) Town where Jesus was born

Answer: Eminem/Bethlehem

6.

a) Christmas chocolate assortment, of which the Malteser is by far the best

b) International inter-governmental organisation founded in 1945

Answer: Celebrations/United Nations

7.

a) What Uri Geller and Dana International are

b) My nan's favourite drink at Christmas, a mix of Irish whiskey and cream

Answer: Israelis/Baileys

8.

a) Baked Christmas treats eaten by Santa

b) Art award won by Grayson Perry and Damien Hirst

Answer: Mince pies/Turner Prize

9.

a) Professor of particle physics and presenter of *Wonders of the Universe*

b) Item of men's underwear that make a traditionally useful, if unimaginative, present

Answer: Brian Cox/Socks

10.

a) Stretch of sand or pebbles where bathers wear no clothes

b) Annual Christmas broadcast from the UK monarch

Answer: Nudist beach/Queen's Speech

11.

a) Vehicle used by Santa

b) UK Prime Minister that no one likes to talk about any more

Answer: Sleigh/(Theresa) May

12.

a) Profession of three of the visitors at the birth of Jesus Christ

b) Animal with the Latin name *Panthera uncia*, which largely lives in mountain ranges

Answer: Shepherd/Snow leopard

13.

a) Traditional fruity accompaniment to turkey

b) Detective created by Colin Dexter

Answer: Cranberry sauce/Inspector Morse

14.

a) Very classy make of men's underpants

b) Cliff Richard's Christmas number one in 1988

Answer: Calvin Klein/'Mistletoe and Wine'

15.

a) Common species of Christmas tree, imported from Scandinavia

b) Host of *Antiques Roadshow* and *Question Time*

Answer: Norway spruce/Fiona Bruce

16.

a) Italian who played for Chelsea and later managed Birmingham City

b) Company often credited with inventing the tradition of Father Christmas dressing in red

Answer: Gianfranco Zola/Coca-Cola

17.

a) Lead singer of the Jam

b) Evergreen Christmas pantomime

Answer: Paul Weller/*Cinderella*

18.

a) **The worst sweet in the Quality Street tin**

b) **Town on the River Usk with slogan 'Gateway to Wales'**

Answer: Toffee penny/Abergavenny

19.

a) **Jolly Christmas song about dashing through snow**

b) **Kent town where Sid Vicious went to school**

Answer: Jingle Bells/Tunbridge Wells

20.

a) **24 December**

b) **Side which won the 2016 UK referendum**

Answer: Christmas Eve/Leave

AC: Psst, readers. Don't tell Richard, but as an extra Christmas present I've been going through the office dictionaries to find him an 'orange' rhyme. There's nothing in Chambers, which is kind of surprising, or in Collins. But I've got up to S in the *Oxford English Dictionary* and I've found something!

It's ... kind of tricky to write a clue for. It's SPORANGE, and it doesn't seem to have been used since it appeared in an 1872 reprint of *Lessons in Elementary Botany: The Part on Systematic Botany Based Upon Material Left in Manuscript by the Late Professor George Henslow*. So that's one problem. On the other hand, it *is* a lovely rhyme.

'Sporange' is a less common form of 'sporangium', and people in the last century and a half seem to prefer saying 'spore-case' instead of even 'sporangium'. So that's another problem. You know what? I'm just going to move on to T. See you much later.

GAME 3

IS IT ME? #1

You need: a chair for each player, pencil and paper
Players: 4 plus someone to read the statements
Scoring: 2 points for every win

Each player stands in front of their chair. The person reading the questions gives them each a piece of paper with the 'thing' that represents them.

As each statement is read out, players remain standing if they think it applies to them and sit down otherwise.

(For the person reading the statements, we've used bold type for the ones where the player should still be standing.)

HEROES OF THE COMICS

Things to write: Batman, Spider-Man, Superman, Wonder Woman

1. I am credited as a character in *The Lego Movie*
   Batman, Spider-Man, **Superman, Wonder Woman**

2. I was orphaned

   Batman, Spider-Man, Superman, Wonder Woman

3. I appear in the *Oxford English Dictionary* other than as a superhero

   Batman, Spider-Man, Superman, Wonder Woman (respectively a butler, a kind of steeplejack, an idealised person of the future and a remarkable female)

4. I wear tights

   Batman, Spider-Man, Superman, Wonder Woman

5. Del Boy attended a wake dressed as me in *Only Fools and Horses*

   Batman, Spider-Man, Superman, Wonder Woman

POPULAR MEATS

Things to write: Beef, pork, chicken,* lamb

1. I am eaten by Harry Potter during his first meal at Hogwarts

   Beef, pork, chicken, lamb

2. I feature in the title of a Best Picture Oscar winner

   Beef, pork, chicken, **lamb**

3. In 2017, the UK exported more of me than it imported

   Beef, pork, chicken, **lamb**

* Poultry also appeared in the very first Is It Me? that we broadcast, memorable for Nish Kumar's belief that chickens produce milk.

4. I feature in the title of a UK number-one single
   Beef, pork, **chicken**, lamb

5. I appear as a verb in the Oxford English Dictionary
   Beef, pork, chicken, lamb

GAME 4
MOUSE OF GAMES #1

You need: nothing
Players: any number, take it in turns
Scoring: 2 for every correct answer

AC: This is one of those games that seems to really go well for whoever's sitting in what we call the Lucky Chair.

RO: The Lucky Chair? You mean the chair where we always and deliberately put the contestant we've booked because we know they're a good quizzer? Often a nerdy comedian?

AC: Yes, the one at the end–

RO: Where we put the person whose job, every day, involves playing with words and finding the exact same kind of appealing turn of phrase that we aim for in this round? Yes, you're right: that contestant does tend to do well in the games involving wordplay.

AC: I know, it's weird, right?

Choose one of the categories. An opposing player will read you a description of a TV show, poem, etc. It is entirely made-up, but it is also a real TV show, poem, etc. *with one letter changed.* So if the description of a novel was 'A pair of beatniks run over a warty amphibian', you would answer not 'On the Road', but 'On the Toad'.

DAYTIME TV, PAST & PRESENT

1. An auction of flats and houses takes place under a large picnic basket.

2. Four amateur chefs provide a meal for Britain's most successful distance runner, a four-time Olympic gold medallist.

3. A heavily tanned antiques expert oversees members of the public haggling to sell sandwiches, crisps and a drink.

4. Andrew Neil and Jo Coburn host a current affairs programme in a TV studio decorated by ornamental lace mats.

5. A flamboyant criminal barrister takes on real-life cases, rewarding successful defendants with a chocolate egg containing a plastic toy.

POEMS

1. Robert Frost recalls with regret not having picked up a warty amphibian.

2. A group of penny-pinching cavalrymen set out 'not to reason why ... but to do and die'.

3. A crazy, aged sailor stops guests from entering a wedding in order to show them a slice of citrus fruit.

4. Dylan Thomas urges a boxer to not be too tender in their upcoming bout.

5. Edgar Allan Poe recounts a chilling tale of being kept awake by a fan of techno music.

Answers:

Daytime TV, Past and Present

1. Homes under the Hamper 2. Come Dine with Mo 3. Dickinson's Meal Deal 4. The Doily Politics 5. Judge Kinder

Poems

1. The Toad Not Taken 2. Charge of the Tight Brigade 3. The Lime of the Ancient Mariner 4. Do Not Go Gentle into that Good Fight 5. The Raver

SET 19 SCORECARD				
	Player 1	Player 2	Player 3	Player 4
Game 1				
Game 2				
Game 3				
Game 4				
Totals				

WINNER!

SET 20

... in which it helps if you know what order the alphabet goes in

GAME 1

IS IT ME? #2

You need: a chair for each player, pencil and paper
Players: 4 plus someone to read the statements
Scoring: 2 points for every win

Each player stands in front of their chair. The person reading the questions gives them each a piece of paper with the 'thing' that represents them.

As each statement is read out, players remain standing if they think it applies to them and sit down otherwise.

(For the person reading the statements, we've used bold type for the ones where the player should still be standing.)

TAKE THAT MEMBERS

Things to write: Gary, Mark, Jason, Howard

1. I am a name found in the King James Bible
   Gary, **Mark, Jason**, Howard

2. I share a first name with one of the founding members of Spandau Ballet
   Gary, Mark, Jason, Howard

3. I am the first name of a footballer who has played for Manchester United in the Premier League
   Gary, Mark, Jason, Howard

4. I am the name of a credited actor in *Harry Potter and the Order of the Phoenix*
   Gary, Mark, Jason, Howard

5. I have sung lead vocals on a Take That single
   Gary, Mark, Jason, **Howard**

FRUITS

Things to write: Plum, melon, pear, banana

1. I am one of the current flavours in Fruit Gums
   Plum, melon, pear, banana

2. I am a source of vitamin C
   Plum, melon, pear, banana

3. **I am an anagram of another fruit that can be found in the *Oxford English Dictionary***

   Plum, **melon**, pear, banana (it's lemon of course)

4. **I was grown on the estates of eighteenth-century British country houses**

   Plum, melon, pear, banana (melons were tricky but those gardeners managed it)

5. **I was used in a 'fruity' remark from Mel and Sue on *The Great British Bake Off***

   Plum, melon, **pear, banana***

* BANANAs were mentioned often in this era, e.g. Sue's 'Or as they would say in Victorian times, wotcha, cock, have a banana.' Mel asked a contestant. 'How do you fan your PLUMs, Alvin?'; she ungrammatically asked another, 'I've got a nice PEAR, Luis - are they soft enough?' MELONs don't tend to feature much in baking.

GAME 2

RIGHT WORDS, WRONG ORDER

You need: your House of Games Spoiler Blocker
Players: any number, take it in turns
Scoring: see below

AC: This is a brilliant game that we've tried out in the *House of Games* HQ, but which hasn't made it on to the screen yet.

RO: There may be a reason for that.

AC: The question writers love it. It takes a good chunk of time to assemble each question, but it's *so* satisfying when it works.

RO: 'A good chunk of time.' Your words, not mine. Don't you lot have a couple of thousand new Answer Smashes to write for the next series? I mean, literally 2,000?

AC: Yes, and spares. Point taken. But let's try Right Words, Wrong Order. Just once.

In this game, the words in the first clue have come out of order.

There are 10 points if you can give the answer based on the mangled clue. If not, move your House of Games Spoiler Blocker down.

There are 5 points if you get it once you know the sort of thing you're looking for.

And there is 1 point if you need the un-mangled clue too.

QUESTION 1

MANGLED CLUE: I was in Australia in the 1990s – I shot an adorable piglet, and boasted.

WHAT YOU'RE LOOKING FOR: title of a film

UNMANGLED CLUE: I was shot in Australia in the 1990s and I boasted an adorable piglet.

Answer: Babe

QUESTION 2

MANGLED CLUE: In the year 2000, I did a number two. For me again, it was ... 'oops!'

WHAT YOU'RE LOOKING FOR: a musician

UNMANGLED CLUE: 'Oops! ... I Did it Again' was a number two for me in the year 2000.

Answer: Britney Spears

QUESTION 3

MANGLED CLUE: I have three arms and legs. My coat has its own language, spoken of by 2,000 of my people.

WHAT YOU'RE LOOKING FOR: part of the British Isles

UNMANGLED CLUE: My coat of arms has three legs. I have my own language and it's spoken by 2,000 of my people.

Answer: The Isle of Man

QUESTION 4

MANGLED CLUE: Am five. I like the books. I have an enormous behind and famous fanbase

WHAT YOU'RE LOOKING FOR: an author

UNMANGLED CLUE: I have an enormous fanbase and I am behind books like *The Famous Five*

Answer: Enid Blyton

RO: 'Just once.' Your words, not mine.

AC: Point taken.

GAME 3

20,8,5 3,15,4,5 7,1,13,5

You need: your House of Games Spoiler Blocker
Players: 2 or more
Scoring: 2 points for the first person to shout each correct answer

This is another game where younger players are especially welcome.

Gather round. All of you. Now, can you all see the page as well as each other?

You can't, can you? Whoever was holding the book is still giving themselves the best view. It's not hard to guess how they behave with a tablet. OK, so jostle a bit.

Right, now we're ready.

Get your House of Games Spoiler Blocker ready and doing its blocking. We're going to show you a category, then some things in that category, with every letter replaced with a number. In this code, 'A's become '1's. 'B's become '2's. 'C's become '3's. 'D's ... well, you've probably cracked the system behind the code.

No buzzers this time. Just howl in each other's ears.

18-5-1-4-25 ...

19-20-5-1-4-25 ...

7-15!

CHILDREN'S SONGS

2,1,1 2,1,1 2,12,1,3,11 19,8,5,5,16

Answer: 'Baa Baa Black Sheep'

8,9,3,11,15,18,25 4,9,3,11,15,18,25 4,15,3,11

Answer: 'Hickory Dickory Dock'

20,23,9,14,11,12,5 20,23,9,14,11,12,5 12,9,20,20,12,5 19,20,1,18

Answer: 'Twinkle Twinkle Little Star'

26,15,15,13 26,15,15,13 26,15,15,13

Answer: 'Zoom Zoom Zoom'

2,1,14,1,14,1,19 9,14 16,25,10,1,13,1,19

Answer: 'Bananas in Pyjamas'

ZOO ANIMALS

2,1,2,15,15,14

Answer: Baboon

5,13,21

Answer: Emu

13,5,5,18,11,1,20

Answer: Meerkat

2,1,20

Answer: Bat

26,5,2,18,1

Answer: Zebra

(A chance for older players to regain some points ...)

HOSTS OF THE BRIT AWARDS

26,15,5 2,1,12,12

Answer: Zoe Ball

4,1,22,9,14,1 13,3,3,1,12,12

Answer: Davina McCall

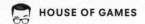

2,5,14 5,12,20,15,14

Answer: Ben Elton

13,9,3,8,1,5,12 1,19,16,5,12

Answer: Michael Aspel

19,1,13,1,14,20,8,1 6,15,24

Answer: Samantha Fox

(And back to a category that's more friendly to those younger players ...)

MONTHS

4,5,3,5,13,2,5,18

Answer: December

10,21,12,25

Answer: July

15,3,20,15,2,5,18

Answer: October

13,1,18,3,8

Answer: March

1,16,18,9,12

Answer: April

GAME 4

THE NICE ROUND - NOVELS

You need: pencil and paper; your House of Games Spoiler Blocker

Players: ideally 4

Scoring: see below

Position your House of Games Spoiler Blocker so that only the first title is visible.

Now, take it in turns to be the Guesser. Each time, everyone who isn't the Guesser reads the answer and writes down a one-word clue to help the Guesser.

After the Guesser has been shown all three clues, they give their guess. They get a point if they're right, and also award a point to whichever player they think has been most helpful.

THE NOVELS

Charlotte's Web

Fahrenheit 451

Sense and Sensibility

Emil and the Detectives

Flat Stanley

The Handmaid's Tale

Crime and Punishment

The Catcher in the Rye

SET 20 SCORECARD				
	Player 1	Player 2	Player 3	Player 4
Game 1				
Game 2				
Game 3				
Game 4				
Totals				

WINNER!

SET 21

... in which a goose fails to make an appearance

GAME 1
MOUSE OF GAMES #2

You need: nothing
Players: any number, take it in turns
Scoring: 2 for every correct answer

AC: You know how we call this game Mouse of Games because it's *House of Games* with a letter changed?

RO: Go on ...

AC: Well, I mean, I think it's great, it's just 'house' to 'mouse' is a bit route-one and–

RO: Alan. We didn't call it Horse of Games. Let it go.

AC: But we *could* change it again! Keep Mouse of Games for now, but then next series, Moose of Games. And the series after that, Goose of Games. And–

RO: Lovely idea. I'll just check with the BBC.

Choose one of the categories. An opposing player will read you a description of a TV show, poem, etc. It is entirely made-up, but it is also a real TV show, poem, etc. *with one letter changed*. So if the description of a BOOK was 'A mole, a rat, a toad and a badger enjoy a chardonnay in the shade of some trees', you would answer not 'The *Wind* in the Willows', but 'The *Wine* in the Willows'.

FAIRY TALES

1. A badly behaved blonde-haired girl breaks into a house and steals a lager, a stout and a pale ale.

2. A former *Strictly* judge becomes increasingly frustrated when no one helps him to bake some bread.

3. The baroque composer of the *Water Music* and his sister are trapped in a gingerbread house by a wicked witch.

4. A total wimp puts on his wellingtons and goes off to see the king.

5. 'You can't catch me!' shouts a Chinese leader made of spiced dough.

HISTORICAL QUOTATIONS (as we all know them)

1. The first man on the moon is astonished to find that a tree with one enormous piece of foliage has grown there.

2. Struck by a musket ball, the captain of HMS *Victory* splutters his dying words to a captain of the England football team.

3. Harry S. Truman takes ultimate responsibility for running his country, insisting that no mallard is getting past the Oval Office.

4. **Marie Antoinette callously remarks that the poor could manage on a diet of cod-like fish.**

5. **Ronald Reagan addresses the Soviet leader and demands that he destroy Moscow's first shopping complex.**

Answers:

Fairy Tales

1. Goldilocks and the Three Beers 2. The Little Red Len 3. Handel and Gretel 4. Wuss in Boots 5. The Gingerbread Mao

Historical Quotations

1. 'That's one small step for man; one giant leaf for mankind' 2. 'Kiss me, Harry 3. 'The duck stops here' 4. 'Let them eat hake' 5. 'Mr. Gorbachev, tear down this mall!'

GAME 2
HOUSE TO GAMES

You need: pencil; perhaps paper
Players: any number
Scoring: 5 points each if you complete it

RO: So I spoke to the BBC about Goose of Games.

AC: That's great, because it looks very much like we could get to Okapi of Games by series 72.

RO: They said it would be confusing for new viewers to be more than one letter away from *House of Games*. They said that Goose of Games doesn't convey what the game *is*, in the same way that Mouse of Games does. Shame.

AC: Richard? When you say 'Lovely idea. I'll just check with the BBC', you don't actually check anything with anyone, do you?

RO: The penny drops. Tell you what'll cheer you up: why don't you use the same idea for a game?

AC: And that's economical, too! Let's do it right now.

Work together on this one. It'll take a while, but you *can* solve it without resorting to your phone.

Every answer is a five-letter word. In the right order, they form a word-chain from HOUSE to GAMES, changing one letter each time.

You will probably get some from the clues, and others once you've started to assemble the chain.

Ice	Every bus has one	Each of them is worth 1⅔ bishops	It's exciting to do this	Harvard dropout of 1975
Tears	Every hotel has these	They're handy in Scrabble	Wipes the floor with	*Dragons' Den* success of 2007

HOUSE

____

____

____

____

____

____

____

____

____

____

GAMES

Answer:
HOUSE
ROUSE (It's exciting to do this)
ROUTE (Every bus has one)
ROUTS (Wipes the floor with)
ROOTS (*Dragons' Den* success of 2007)
ROOKS (Each of them is worth 1⅔ bishops)
ROCKS (Ice)
RACKS (They're handy in Scrabble)
RACES (Tears)
RATES (Every hotel has these)
GATES (Harvard dropout of 1975)
GAMES

GAME 3
AMERICAN PUZZLE TIME

You need: pencil
Players: any number
Scoring: 20 points each if you complete it

RO: That word-chain was fun. Not purely general knowledge, but not just definitions.

AC: It's the way they clue American crosswords. You're not expected to get most of the clues straightaway, but when the words start to fit together, it starts making sense. For example ...

RO: You've been working on one, haven't you?

ACROSS

1. Biological bag
4. 'Oh for heaven's sake, not you as well, Brutus!?'
5. Galaxy's replacement, perhaps
6. 'Today!'
7. Stuff that lubricates blades

DOWN

1. One of 1.8m used every day in the UK (until recently)
2. On
3. Beaver's bigger brother?
4. No worries
5. One to swipe left on

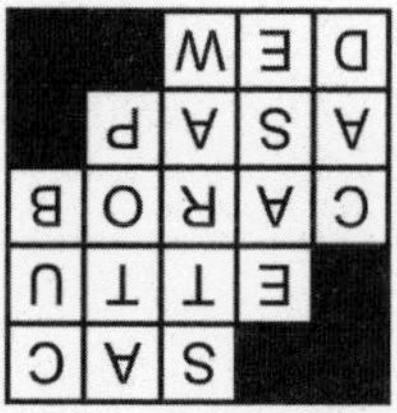

GAME 4
CORRECTION CENTRE #2

You need: buzzers, or noise-makers of some sort
Players: any number, plus someone to read out the nonsense
Scoring: 2 for every correct answer

RO: These questions seem dimly familiar …

AC: Yep! They're the Correction Centres that we wrote when we first came up with the idea for the show. Three years ago now.

RO: The heady days of development. We hadn't found a shape for the show then, but we knew that the contestants would stay all week, that the games would keep changing …

AC: … and that there were to be absolutely no members of the public in the studio. I remember you could not have been clearer about that.

RO: Yes, well, if you have an audience, it's a much longer day, and I didn't think that would be fair on the crew.

AC: Sure. That was the reason.

Take it in turns to read these statements aloud. Each of them is completely untrue. Buzz in when you know how changing *just one word* in the sentence will make it accurate.

1. The model Jordan is more than 300 kilometres long.

2. In the sitcom *Blackadder*, Baldrick was played by Smokey Robinson.

3. Brazil were finalists in the 1998 World Cup, but lost to Cowdenbeath.

4. King Charles II appointed John Lydon as the first Poet Laureate.

5. One of Leonardo da Vinci's most famous works is The Last Cuppa.

6. Ellen DeGeneres is the hero of Ridley Scott's 1979 film, *Alien*.

7. The opening words of Herman Melville's novel *Moby Dick* are 'Call me, babe'.

8. The 1904 agreement between Britain and France is known as the Elderflower Cordiale.

9. In the nineteenth century, the Anglo-Zanzibar war lasted around 38 years.

10. Between Uranus and Pluto is the planet Tatooine.

11. *Bonus rejected question, avoid if you are squeamish:*
    The Panama Canal is made up, from end to end, of muscle, mucosa and connective tissue.

AC: I can't remember why that last one was rejected. Maybe there was more than one correct answer?

RO: Or possibly, just possibly, we didn't think the BBC would be enthusiastic about making viewers picture 50 miles of human gore during a teatime quiz.

Answers:

1. The **River** Jordan is more than 300 kilometres long.
2. In the sitcom Blackadder, Baldrick was played by **Tony** Robinson.
3. Brazil were finalists in the 1998 World Cup, but lost to **France**.
4. King Charles II appointed John **Dryden** as the first Poet Laureate of the UK.
5. One of Leonardo da Vinci's most famous works is The Last **Supper**.
6. Ellen **Ripley** is the hero of Ridley Scott's 1979 film, *Alien*.
7. The opening words of Herman Melville's novel *Moby Dick* are 'Call me **Ishmael**'.
8. The 1904 agreement between Britain and France is known as the **Entente** Cordiale.
9. In the nineteenth century, the Anglo-Zanzibar war lasted around 38 **minutes**.
10. Between Uranus and Pluto is the planet **Neptune**.

11 The **alimentary** canal is made up of 30 feet of muscle, mucosa and connective tissue.

SET 21 SCORECARD				
	Player 1	Player 2	Player 3	Player 4
Game 1				
Game 2				
Game 3				
Game 4				
Totals				

WINNER!

SET 22

... in which you will imagine life in the year 2041

GAME 1

THE ANSWER'S IN THE QUESTION #2

You need: a smartphone or tablet; your House of Games Spoiler Blocker
Players: any number
Scoring: see below

AC: Almost all of the questions in this book are brand new, but we simply had to include these Answer's In The Question sets because, after we played them in the studio, our host paused to lead *a round of applause* for the questions, prompting the question-writing team to remark ,'You don't get that from [redacted]', '[redacted] never did this' and '[redacted] regards the questions as a nuisance.'

In fact, now seems a good moment to mention the fine people who wrote the actual questions which make up the book and TV show, rather than squishing everyone in at the end: James Allison, Tom Banks, Abby Brakewell, Katie Burns, Andrew Credgington, Rose Dawson, the Dawson Brothers, Carl Earl-Ocran, James Ellis, Reece Finnegan, Becky Gardner, Joe Gardner, Elliott Howarth-Johnson, Samuel Jones, Ben Justice, Rebecca Kidger, Danny Lorimer, Stephen Lovelock, Sam Munday, Josh Pemberton, Mark Porter, Sophie Reid, Josephine Sarchet, Sam Shepherd, Bethany Steed, Laura Watson and of course Jack Yeo.

Talking of heroes often unsung, let's also include the *spare* questions for each set, yeah?

In this game, we've been generous enough to give you a clue *and* the answer.

In case you don't find the simple act of reading the answer aloud satisfying, we've jumbled them up. The words in **bold type** can be jumbled up to give each answer, which is also described by the clue as a whole.

You'll probably want to gather round the book and do this together. But if you insist, someone can read them out and you can get competitive.

SHAKESPEARE PLAYS

1. This tragedy opens with the title character dividing his realm between his **regal kin**.
2. This play's **writer somehow finds very** many ways to embarrass its lead character, Sir John Falstaff.
3. This **rotten anaconda play** ends with the heroine using a snake to poison herself.
4. **This man of note** is the title character of a tragedy set in Greece.
5. In this play, Leontes sends his lords across **the silent water** to the Isle of Delphos.

HISTORICAL FIGURES

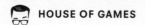

1. **Angel of the Reclining** is a good nickname for this nineteenth-century social reformer.

2. **Casual juries** would never have convicted this general, so his enemies decided to take more drastic action.

3. Because he was a **gawky fuse**-lighter, he was caught red-handed.

4. **Ye pump sales** may have increased dramatically after the Great Fire of London, witnessed by this diarist.

5. This playwright was riding high in Victorian society until his private life **drew social** criticism.

Answers:

Shakespeare plays

1. *King Lear* 2. *The Merry Wives of Windsor* 3. *Antony and Cleopatra* 4. *Timon of Athens* 5. *The Winter's Tale*

Historical figures

1. Florence Nightingale 2. Julius Caesar 3. Guy Fawkes 4. Samuel Pepys 5. Oscar Wilde

GAME 2

AND THE ANSWER ISN'T #7

You need: a smartphone or tablet; your House of Games Spoiler Blocker

Players: ideally 4; you could make it work with 2 but it's probably not worth it

Scoring: see below

These four questions are multiple-choice, but we haven't bothered to come up with the wrong ones. That's your job.

When it's your turn, everyone else looks at the question and its answer. Then (so that handwriting is no clue), someone takes the phone and types in (in random order) the right answer and a multi-choice option from each of the other players. (You shouldn't also type in any of the fun facts we offer as explanation.)

Then you get the phone, someone reads you the question, and you consider the options.

If you're right, you get a point. Obviously. But if you're wrong, the point goes to whoever invented the option you chose. Take your time …

1. **Why did the Russian Olympic shooting team arrive 12 days late for the London 1908 Olympic Games?**

   Answer: They were using the Julian Calendar

2. **In 2018, archaeologists discovered the only known example of what Roman artefact at a fort on Hadrian's Wall?**

   Answer: Boxing gloves (which still have knuckle imprints from a luckless ancient fighter)

3. **What is the scientific name for the Western Lowland Gorilla?**

   Answer: *Gorilla gorilla*

4. **What was particularly unusual about Jack the Signalman, who worked at a Cape Town train station in the late nineteenth century?**

   Answer: He was a baboon (the original signalman lost his legs in an accident and acquired the baboon to help him with his work)

GAME 3
GREAT DOUBLE ACTS

You need: nothing
Players: any number, take it in turns
Scoring: 5 for every correct pair of answers

RO: Hey, what happened to that idea of mine, Great Double Acts?

AC: I'll show you now.

RO: We haven't done it in studio ...?

AC: It's such a good idea, we saved it for the book.

Below are the names of some notable pairs – simply choose the right options to make up that pair.

LAUREL & HARDY

First, choose which of these images shows laurel leaves:

A

B

Next, choose which of these writers is Thomas Hardy:

C

D

Finally, say 'A&C', 'A&D', 'B&C' or 'B&D' to your opponent and ask them to look up what you've chosen.

Got the idea? Great!

MORECAMBE & WISE

First, which arrow points to Morecambe?

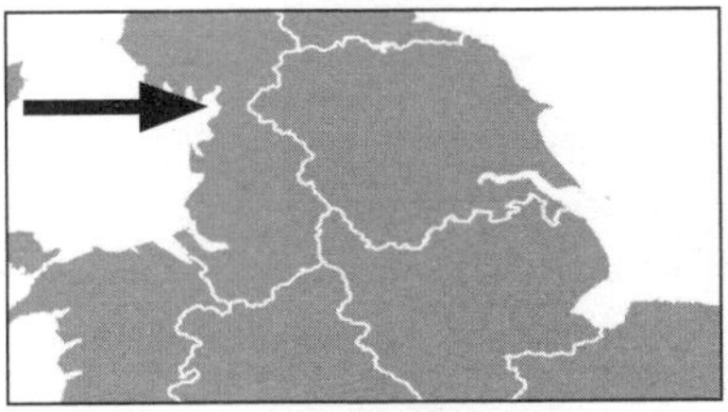

A

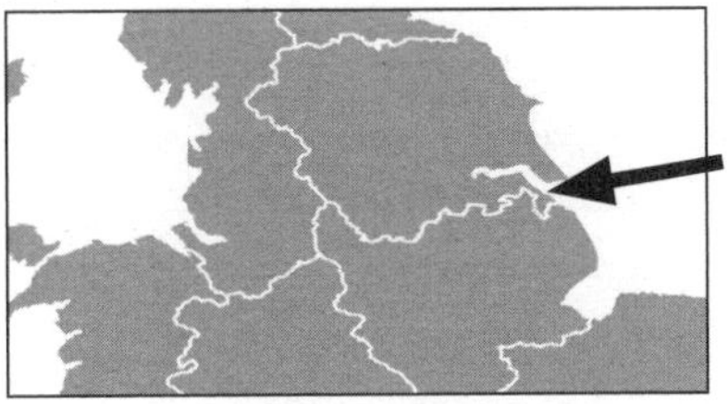

B

And where did Dennis Wise play?

C

D

Tell your opponent your choice and hand over the book ...

LITTLE & LARGE

Which of these arrows points to the Little Bear, also known as Ursa Minor?

A

B

And which of these maps is drawn to a large scale?

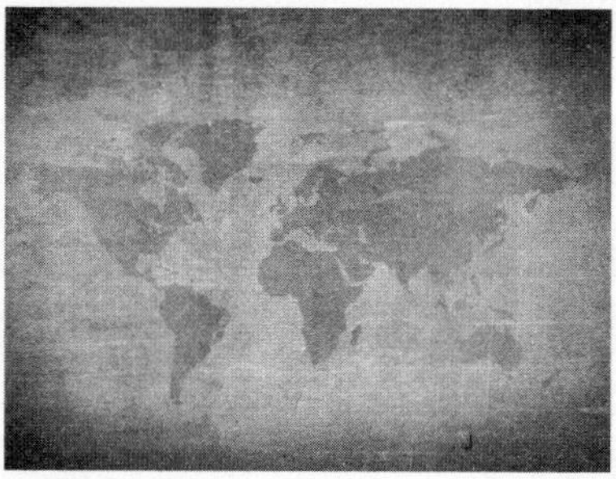

C

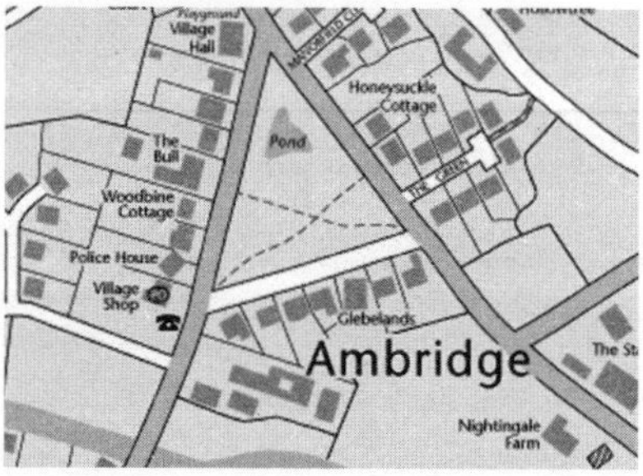

D

TOM & JERRY

Which of these characters from *The Good Life* is Tom?

A

B

Finally, when they started out, Simon & Garfunkel called themselves Tom & Jerry (their stage names were 'Tom Graph', reflecting one singer's love of maths, and 'Jerry Landis', a reference to the other one's girlfriend). Which was Jerry?

C

D

Answers:

Laurel & Hardy
A&C: Laburnum & Hardy A&D: Laburnum & Dickens B&C: Laurel & Hardy B&D: Laurel & Dickens

Morecambe & Wise
A&C: Morecambe & Wise A&D: Morecambe & Zola B&C: Grimsby & Wise B&D: Grimsby & Zola

Little & Large
A&C: Great & Small A&D: Great & Large B&C: Little & Small B&D: Little & Large

Tom & Jerry
A&C: Tom & Jerry A&D: Tom & Tom B&C: Jerry & Jerry B&D: Jerry & Tom

GAME 4

DISTINCTLY AVERAGE #3

You need: pencil and paper; a phone, or someone who's good with numbers

Players: 4, 6, 8, 10 ... basically, an even number that's 4 or more

Scoring: 2 points for every win

Sort yourselves into pairs.

For the rules, see Game 2, Page 18: A Distinctly Average Christmas. This is one, though, that you can play at any time of year. (We said that last time, but we've realised you can also play the Christmas one any time of year too. As you were.)

1. **According to the Office for National Statistics, how many working days were lost due to sickness or injury in the UK in 2016?**

2. **According to a 2015 study by the journal *Nature*, how many trees are there in the world?**

3. **How many times does the word 'goat' appear in the King James version of the Bible?**

4. **According to the Office for National Statistics, what is the predicted population of the UK in 2041?**

5. **According to the official royal website, approximately how many cups of tea are consumed at each of the Queen's Garden Parties?**

Answers:
1. 137,300,000
2. 3,040,000,000,000 (to the nearest 40 billion)
3. 128 (one has a conspicuous horn between his eyes)
4. 72,900,000
5. 27,000, so it's important to go to the loo *before* you arrive

SET 22 SCORECARD				
	Player 1	Player 2	Player 3	Player 4
Game 1				
Game 2				
Game 3				
Game 4				
Totals				

WINNER!

SET 23

... in which you will be looked at by a fish

GAME 1

AND THE ANSWER ISN'T – THE QUOTATIONS VERSION

You need: a smartphone or tablet; your House of Games Spoiler Blocker

Players: ideally 4; you could make it work with 2 but it's probably not worth it

Scoring: see below

These four questions are multiple-choice, but we haven't bothered to come up with the wrong ones. That's your job.

When it's your turn, everyone else looks at the quotation. Then (so that handwriting is no clue), someone takes the phone and types in the start of the quotation, and then (in random order) the right ending and a multi-choice option from each of the other players.

Then you get the phone, they tell you who said the quotation, and you consider the options.

If you're right, you get a point. Obviously. But if you're wrong, the point goes to whoever invented the option you chose. Take your time ...

1. Erma Bombeck:

   'There is nothing sadder in this world than ...

   ... to awake Christmas morning and not be a child.'

2. Benjamin Franklin:

   'A good conscience ...

   ... is a continual Christmas.'

(The hidden theme should now be apparent.)

3. Mr Elton in Jane Austen's *Emma*:

   'At Christmas every body invites their friends about them, and people think little of ...

   ... even the worst weather.'

4. Winston Churchill:

   'Christmas is a season not only of rejoicing ...

   ... but of reflection.'

5. Nick Hornby's *About a Boy*:

   'It struck him that how you spent Christmas ...

   ... was a message to the world about where you were in life.'

GAME 2
RYDER CUP OR LIE-DER CUP?

You need: possibly a phone and/or pencil and paper
Players: any number, split into two teams
Scoring: 1 point for every correct answer

RO: Below are two teams of 12 golfers. Half of each team are real, and half are names I've just made up. But who is who?

Each team should take Team A and eventually come to an agreement on which are the real golfers. (One team can take a photo of this page.)

TEAM A

(Six of these players are real, and six are fake)

Fred Funk
Peter Prix
Luke List
Kelly Kraft
Don Drizzell
Robert Rock
Tom Trunk
Steve Stricker

Jimmy Jackle

Mike Mulch

Campbell Cardinal

Bronson Burgoon

TEAM B

(A bit harder now. Or is it easier? You tell me. Nine of these are real golfers. Can you spot the three fakes?)

Kirk Triplett

Dicky Pride

Curtis Strange

Billy Shoe

Jeff Maggert

Jason Kokrak

Larry Laurie

Jodie Mudd

Mighty González

Fuzzy Zoeller

Wiffy Cox

Boo Weekley

Answers:

Team A

Real: Fred Funk, Luke List, Kelly Kraft, Robert Rock, Steve Stricker, Bronson Burgoon

Fake: Peter Prix, Don Drizzell, Tom Trunk, Jimmy Jackle, Mike Mulch, Campbell Cardinal

Team B

Real: Kirk Triplett, Dicky Pride, Curtis Strange, Jeff Maggert, Jason Kokrak, Jodie Mudd, Fuzzy Zoeller, Wiffy Cox, Boo Weekley

Fake: Billy Shoe, Larry Laurie, Mighty González

GAME 3
HOUSE OF GALES #3

You need: nothing
Players: any number, take it in turns
Scoring: 2 for every correct answer

Choose one of the categories. An opposing player will read you a description of a TV show, poem, etc. It is entirely made-up, but it is also a real TV show, poem, etc. *with one letter changed*. So if the description of a musical was 'A runaway orphan pickpockets garnishes for a Martini', you would answer not 'Oliver!', but 'Olives!'

FAMOUS PAINTINGS

1. In a half-length portrait, a talking bird looks out with a sideways glance and an enigmatic smile.
2. Long after sunset, the sky explodes with colour, illuminating a cypress tree and a punch-up.
3. A fish gazes over its shoulder at you, wearing a blue-and-yellow headdress, with a large piece of jewellery stuck in its respiratory organ.
4. A goddess stands in an enormous shell with a wine list in one had and a pudding list in the other.
5. In a dining hall in Jerusalem, 13 men compete in a race to consume all the wine and unleavened bread.

BOB DYLAN SONGS

1. A small cake topped with jam and cream tumbles down a hillside.

2. A series of gnomic questions can only be answered by making bubbles appear in a glass of merlot.

3. A troupe of performers get into costume, ready for a show in which no words are spoken.

4. A joker and a thief enjoy some hoppy quaffs at the top of a lookout station.

5. Covered by Adele, in this song Dylan coaxes the listener to stroke his white bird which resembles a pigeon.

Answers:

Famous Paintings
1. (The) Myna Lisa 2. The Starry Fight 3. Gill with a Pearl Earring 4. The Birth of Menus 5. The Fast Supper*

Bob Dylan Songs
1. Like a Rolling Scone 2. Blowin' in the Wine 3. The Mimes They Are A-Changin' 4. Ale Along the Watchtower 5. Make You Feel My Dove

---

* A Cambridge professor has recently worked out that the Last Supper was on a Wednesday.

GAME 4

5, 4, 3, 2, 1

You need: to know your own age
Players: any number, younger players very welcome
Scoring: see below

The youngest player starts and tries to answer the FIVE question, with a point for each of the five correct answers. If they get them all right, they get to try the FOUR question; if not, play passes to the next player.

(By the way, if you get any of the answers in the correct order, from left to right, double your score.)

FIVE

Name the colours of the five rings on the Olympic flag

Answer: From left to right: blue, yellow, black, green and red

FOUR

Name the four colours in Google's logo

Answer: From left to right: blue, red, yellow, green

THREE

Name the three colours on the Belgian flag

Answer: From left to right: black, yellow, red

TWO

Name the two colours on the classic Faber-Castell rubber (positioned with the writing the right way up, the pencil eraser is on the left and the pen eraser on the right)

Answer: Red, blue

ONE

Name the one colour of Mr Lazy

Answer: Pink

SET 23 SCORECARD				
	Player 1	Player 2	Player 3	Player 4
Game 1				
Game 2				
Game 3				
Game 4				
Totals				

WINNER!

SET 24

... in which one of you may be asked to leave the room

GAME 1

ESAELP SREWSNA

You need: your House of Games Spoiler Blocker; a stopwatch (most likely on a phone, unless you're a PE teacher or hoarder of obsolete devices – and what else have you got in the drawer where you keep your stopwatch? A dictaphone?)

Players: any number

Scoring: 10 points for the winner

Take it in turns to ask each other the stacks of questions below. They're not too tricky, but you only get the next question (and the point) if you can give the answer *backwards*. So if the question is 'What kind of beer is a pilsner?', you would *think* 'lager' but *say* 'regal'.

When it's your turn to ask the questions, time how long it takes the other player to answer the stack. Add 10 seconds for anything they get wrong and 20 seconds if they ever give the actual answer, rather than the backwards one.

Ready?

STACK ONE

1. The Three Little Pigs built their houses from bricks, sticks ... and what?

   Answer: Warts

2. And what kind of animal is trying to eat them?

   Answer: Flow

3. **What electric vehicles provide public transport in Sheffield, Edinburgh and Manchester?**

   Answer: Smart

4. **What is the name of the brother of Oasis's Noel Gallagher?**

   Answer: Mail

5. **Alpha Centauri A, Sirius B and our own sun are examples of what heavenly body?**

   Answer: Rats

STACK TWO

1. **The three wires in a plug are earth, neutral ... and what?**

   Answer: Evil

2. **Which real-life public school was attended by Captain Hook, Bertie Wooster and James Bond?**

   Answer: Note

3. **In the *Beano*, which 'Menace' is the owner and friend of Gnasher?**

   Answer: Sinned

4. **Street View is a feature of which Google service?**

   Answer: Spam

5. **In the abbreviation TGI Friday, what does the G stand for?**

   Answer: Dog

STACK THREE

1. 4,480 pounds is the same as two ... what?

   Answer: Snot

2. What was the name of the German boy detective in the 1929 story by Erich Kästner?

   Answer: Lime

3. What canal joins the Red Sea to the Med?

   Answer: Zeus

4. In the kitchen, 'soup', 'wooden' and 'measuring' are all what?

   Answer: Snoops

5. What word, often combined with 'Avon', is used to describe William Shakespeare?

   Answer: Drab

STACK FOUR

1. What four-letter word appears in white on a red, octagonal road sign?

   Answer: Pots

2. What material is usually used to make jeans?

   Answer: Mined

3. What is the surname of the tramp known as 'Mister' in David Walliams's story?

   Answer: Knits

4. Unagi, moray and conger: these are three types of what?

Answer: Lee

5. A 1980s craze involved doing a 'hula'-like dance while trying to keep a *what* from landing on the ground?

Answer: Pooh

RO: That was fun. Let's do that on the telly. And have you seen my glasses?

AC: No point. There's only so many words that are other words backwards, and you try coming up with a question for STRESSED.

RO: Let's see ... `What Richard Osman is never known to be, even at the end of a long day in studio.'

AC: Right! But we'd also need clues for AVID and ERGO. Right?

RO: Wait. Why are you being nice?

AC: I'm sitting on your glasses.

GAME 2

IMAGINARY CHARADES #2

You need: your House of Games Spoiler Blocker
Players: any number; make 2 teams or just take it in turns to act out the titles
Scoring: 20 points for whoever has made the bravest choices and moves

Look around the room. Is anyone the kind of person who'll say 'I *just* don't under*stand* this', when faced with something that's perfectly easy to understand and just ... well, fun?

Ask them to leave.

Have they gone? Good.

Now you're ready for Imaginary Charades. Normal rules and conventions, and use your House of Games Spoiler Blocker to cover up the titles below; the only difference is that none of the things you'll be acting out actually exists.

TITLES

(younger players: if you don't know some of the names and words, just make up your own title instead)

The Scottish Park-Keeper (play)

The Archbishop Was Poisoned on Tuesday (book)

Grimacing Is as Grimacing Does (TV show)

You Ain't No Genius, Neil Armstrong (play)

Patience, Prudence (song)

Yes I Do, No I Don't, Oh What's the Point? (book)

Queuing for Pretzels (film)

Hyundai Amica Madness (TV show)

Kangaroo II: Kangaroo Boogaloo (film)

Between Indigo and Maroon, Between Burgundy and Magenta (play)

GAME 3
HOUSE OF GAMPS #4

You need: buzzers, or noise-makers of some sort
Players: any number, plus someone to read out the nonsense
Scoring: 2 points for every correct answer

Choose one of the categories. An opposing player will read you a description of a TV show, poem, etc. It is entirely made-up, but it is also a real TV show, poem, etc. *with one letter changed*. So if the description of a children's TV character was 'An incorrigible red fox makes mischief in a Swiss city on the Rhine', you would answer not 'Basil Brush', but 'Basel Brush'.

QUEEN SONGS

1. Freddie celebrates a female deer which performs conjuring tricks.

2. Freddie finds the proportion between two numbers absolutely insane.

3. Freddie wishes ill upon a Manchester United midfielder from Brazil.

4. Freddie announces the winners of a jam-making contest.

5. Freddie asks not to be put in an overhead locker quite yet.

ELTON JOHN SONGS

1. Sir Elton celebrates a deaf, dumb and blind reptile.

2. Sir Elton imagines himself as an astronaut with a vitamin D deficiency.

3. Sir Elton wistfully pictures *X Factor* winner Matt stuck in a gale.

4. Sir Elton hopes that Attila's Persian campaign will prove a success.

5. Sir Elton teaches British terms to Americans, but they can't get the hang of what we call their 'truck'.

Answers:

Queen Songs

1. It's a Hind of Magic 2. Ratio Gaga 3. I Want to Break Fred 4. WI Are the Champions 5. Don't Stow Me Now

Elton John Songs

1. Pinball Lizard 2. Ricket Man 3. Cardle in the Wind 4. Don't Let the Hun Go Down on Me 5. Lorry Seems to Be the Hardest Word

GAME 4

$^2/_3$ OF THE AVERAGE

You need: a phone each
Players: more than 2
Scoring: 20 points for whoever wins most often

Only play this game if you have already played Game 2, Page 72: 5, 6, 7, 8.

Like in 5, 6, 7, 8, each of you taps a number into your phone – this time anything from 0 to 100.

And this time, whoever has tapped the highest number then presses + and adds everyone else's number, then ÷ 3 and finally =.

Whoever's original number is closest to the number that comes up is the winner. And *that's* why it's called $^2/_3$ Of The Average.

And once you've finished ... you play it again.

SET 24 SCORECARD				
	Player 1	Player 2	Player 3	Player 4
Game 1				
Game 2				
Game 3				
Game 4				
Totals				

WINNER!

SET 25

... in which you have your last chance to vanquish your mortal foes (friends and family)

GAME 1

HIGHBROW LOWBROW – THE ACTUAL GAME #3

You need: your House of Games Spoiler Blocker
Players: 2 pairs
Scoring: see below

When it's your pair's turn to answer, ask one of the other pair to read you one of the Highbrow Questions. If you get it right, that's 5 points. If you don't, ask them to read the Lowbrow Question.

The answer is the same, but if you need both, you get only 1 point.

HIGHBROW: Which actor played Vladimir alongside Ian McKellen's Estragon in *Waiting for Godot*?

LOWBROW: Which actor played Poop alongside Christina Aguilera's Akiko Glitter in *The Emoji Movie*?

Answer: Patrick Stewart

HIGHBROW: Which country was led by President Ólafur Ragnar Grímsson from 1996 until 2016?

LOWBROW: Which retailer was the sponsor of *I'm a Celebrity … Get Me Out of Here!* from 2004 until 2014?

Answer: Iceland

HIGHBROW: What is the usual English translation of the title of Albert Camus's philosophical novel *La Chute*?

LOWBROW: In November 2005, the results on *Final Score* were read by the lead singer of which Manchester band?

Answer: The Fall

HIGHBROW: At Oxford and Cambridge universities, what term is used for the officials who assist the proctors in disciplinary matters?

LOWBROW: On *Celebrity Juice*, what are Gary and Spud?

Answer: Bulldogs (or rather 'what *was*', for Gary, who sadly passed away in 2012)

HIGHBROW: Which fruit, native to Brazil, is also known by the Latin name *Passiflora edulis*?

LOWBROW: What fruit is the title of a leisurely R&B house groove by Drake?

Answer: Passionfruit

HIGHBROW: In May 1862, during the American Civil War, the Virginia town to which General Nathaniel P. Banks retreated was called ... what?

LOWBROW: In *Shaun of the Dead*, during the battle with the zombies, the local pub to which Shaun and his friends retreat is called the ... what?

Answer: Winchester

GAME 2

FIVES ALIVE - YOUNGER PLAYERS' EDITION

You need: nothing
Players: any number
Scoring: no points - work together

This works in just the same way as the previous Fives Lives: from the first letters of the answers, guess each of these top fives.

A) JOBS MOST CHILDREN WOULD LIKE WHEN THEY GROW UP

1 T

2 V

3 D

F

5 P(O)

B) MOST COMMON* NAMES GIVEN TO ROYAL BABIES IN LAST 200 YEARS

1 A

2 G

3 V

4 C

5 E and M (fifth-place tie)

C) BIRDS MOST OFTEN SEEN IN BRITISH GARDENS

1 S

2 S

3 B T

4 B

5 P

D) SURNAMES OF 'CLASSIC' CHILDREN'S AUTHORS (AS IN, THEY ARE ALL DEAD) MOST BORROWED FROM UK LIBRARIES

1 D

2 B

3 P

4 L

5 C

---

* Not that kind of common.

E) MOST COMMON* NAMES FOR PETS

1 A

2 P

3 M

4 C

5 M

Answers:

A) Teacher, Vet, Doctor, Footballer (not firefighter!), Police officer (Source: Hoop)
B) Albert, George, Victoria, Charles, Edward and Mary (Source: Expedia)
C) Sparrow (technically house sparrow), starling, blue tit, blackbird, pigeon (technically woodpigeon) (Source: RSPB Big Garden Birdwatch 2018)
D) Dahl, Blyton, Potter, Lewis, Carroll (Source: Public Lending Right data at the British Library)
E) Alfie, Poppy, Molly, Charlie, Max (Source: Protect Your Bubble)

* No comment.

GAME 3

SEE MY GUESTS #7&8

You need: your House of Games Spoiler Blocker
Players: any number (and someone to check your guesses)
Scoring: see below

In this game, you work together.

You'll see two images of guests from the TV version of *House of Games*. If you can tell who they are straightaway, that's *10 points each*. (Get someone else to check, in case you're wrong.)

If you can't, then there are some nice straightforward questions underneath, of the kind we use in our round It's All In The Name. As that name suggests, this will give you some of the letters of the guest's name. But each time you use one of these questions, *the points available go down by 2*.

Cooperation and inspiration: and you'll all boost your scores.

GUEST SEVEN

For 10 points:

Can you name her?

Answer these questions to get some of the letters in her name.

For 8 points:

Dennis the Menace's pet pig in *The Beano*

Answer: Rasher (the Abyssinian wire-haired tripe hound is called Gnasher)

For 6 points:

Surname of the Premier League's all-time top goal scorer

Answer: Shearer

For 4 points:

Animals depicted as Disney's Gus and Luke, and John Burningham's Borka

Answer: Geese

For 2 points:

What the grass always is on the other side of the fence

Answer: Greener

Answers: Sarah Greene

GUEST EIGHT

For 10 points:

Can you name him?

Answer these questions to get some of the letters in his name.

For 8 points:

Olympic event using a blunted sword

Answer: Épée (but his name doesn't have the exotic accents)

For 6 points:

Second longest river in British Isles (after Shannon)

Answer: Severn

For 4 points:

Month that America holds its presidential elections

Answer: November

For 2 points:

Month that party conference season begins

Answer: September

Answers: Steve Pemberton

GAME 4
SMASHING CAROLS

You need: your House of Games Spoiler Blocker; to know and hopefully enjoy Christmas carols
Players: any number
Scoring: 1 for each correct smash; 2 if you sing the answer; no points if you fail to smash

RO: You're looking happy. That can only mean ...

AC: ... yep. It's the second festive Answer Smash, and this time, we've followed *every single rule*.

The questions come in pairs: on the *left* is a line from a Christmas carol and on the *right* is a clue to another answer. You have to smash the name of the carol into the other answer. So if the clues were `Fa, la, la, la, la, la, la, la, la!' and `Flavouring used in Jamaican cuisine', you would answer DECK THE HALLSPICE.

You can take it in turns, or have someone read them out with everyone else on 'buzzers'.

Got it? Let's smash.

1	Round yon Virgin, Mother and Child Holy infant so tender and mild	Terrifying 1968 zombie movie
2	Mary was that mother mild Jesus Christ her little child	A nice short holiday in Paris, Rome or Bruges, say
3	On a cold winter's night That was so deep	Composer of the soundtrack to *The Lion King*
4	And Heaven and nature sing, and Heaven and nature sing And Heaven, and Heaven, and nature sing	Computer game that takes place in Azeroth, or something like that
5	Above thy deep and dreamless sleep The silent stars go by	Hertfordshire new town with initials H.H. that Roger Moore made his home
6	When the snow lay round about Deep and crisp and even	Baked pasta dish favoured by Garfield the cat
7	Earth stood hard as iron Water like a stone	Indomitable football team whose home is San Siro
8	Westward leading, still proceeding Guide us to thy perfect light	Railway station with a Platform 9¾
9	Oh tidings of comfort and joy, comfort and joy Oh tidings of comfort and joy	Funny 1953 musical with Jane Russell *and* Marilyn Monroe
10	Glo-oh-oh-oh-oh-oh, oh-oh-oh-oh-oh-oh, oh-oh-oh-oh-oh-oh, oh-oh-oh-oh-oh-oh, oh-oh-oh-oh-oh-oh-oria	Fascinating book that tells you what road signs mean

Answers: 1. Silent Night of the Living Dead 2. Once in Royal David's City Break 3. The First Noelton John 4. Joy to the World of Warcraft 5. O Little Town of Bethlehemel Hempstead 6. Good King Wenceslasagne 7. In the Bleak Midwinter Milan 8. We Three Kings Cross 9. God Rest Ye Merry, Gentlemen Prefer Blondes 10. Ding Dong Merrily on Highway Code

SET 25 SCORECARD				
	Player 1	Player 2	Player 3	Player 4
Game 1				
Game 2				
Game 3				
Game 4				
Totals				

WINNER!

___

GAME #101
WIN SWAG

You need: the internet, probably
Players: any number
Scoring: not applicable

AC: It's the end of a quiz. And that means prizes.

RO: Um, yes. Readers, feel free to award the winner something. An unwanted Secret Santa gift that no one in your family has owned up to having bought, perhaps.

AC: I thought perhaps … we could give a prize?

RO: A very generous thought, Alan. Do I have to do anything?

AC: Not until Christmas. Readers, your challenge is this: to identify the only (I think this is right) guest on *House of Games* who could be *both halves* of an Answer Smash answer. Now, here's a quick reminder of what makes an Answer Smash …

RO: I knew it. This is really a pretext for going on about the 'rules'.

AC: … the first half and the second half need to overlap by at least three letters. The smashed answer needs to be easy to say aloud, and you *must* remember to check the database to see if it's been used before. Brand names probably won't make it through …

RO: Alan, this is not a briefing for new question-writers.

AC: Ah, yes. Once you've worked out which guest we're talking about, tweet the name to @richardosman using the hashtag #ROHOGbook. The first three of you to get it right will get something left over from the *House of Games* range of prizes and–

RO: Alan, you've worked in TV. You remember the great Competition Controversies of 2008. There are reams of documents specifically to deny such simple pleasures.

AC: Right. Well, the winners will get the Keys to the House of Games.

RO: And these keys have no tangible value or potential for financial exchange?

AC: No, no. They're just words.

RO: This has been fun.

AC: It has! I must remember to thank James Fox, Dom Waugh, Rich Hague, Susan King, Sarah Boyce and everyone else at Remarkable; Yvonne Jacob, Charlotte Macdonald, Howard Watson, Toby Clarke, Albert DePetrillo and everyone else at BBC Books; Alice Bernardi, Susie Chase, Penny Roberts and the legal team at Endemol Shine UK ...

RO: ... *don't* forget the commissioners ...

AC: ... Alex McLeod, Dan McGolpin and everyone else at BBC Daytime and Early-Peak. But most especially our magnificent executive producer Tamara Gilder. Pint?

RO: I think we could pop in to the Guilderman's.

AC: Actually, I was thinking of the Lovelock Arms. I know it's a slightly further walk, but, um ...

RO: There's a quiz there tonight, isn't there?

AC: Jackpot's rolled over to 30 quid. And it's the only one we haven't been barred from.

FINAL SCORECARD

Tick off the winner of each set, and declare the overall House of Games Champion! Bonus points all round if you also tot up your individual points scores.

	Player 1	Player 2	Player 3	Player 4
Set 1				
Set 2				
Set 3				
Set 4				
Set 5				
Set 6				
Set 7				
Set 8				
Set 9				
Set 10				
Set 11				
Set 12				
Set 13				
Set 14				
Set 15				
Set 16				
Set 17				
Set 18				
Set 19				
Set 20				
Set 21				
Set 22				
Set 23				
Set 24				
Set 25				
TOTAL:				

HOUSE OF GAMES SPOILER BLOCKER

Did you think that we would let you play without your own customised avatar like the ones in See My Guests? Shame on you. At House of Games, we put you first. Here they are!*

AVATAR #1

* Obviously you have to draw these

AVATAR #2

AVATAR #3

AVATAR #4